(WELL) CONNECTED ARCHITECTURE

(WELL) CONNECTED ARCHITECTURE
IAN RITCHIE

ACADEMY EDITIONS • ERNST & SOHN

Although it has been my responsibility to write this book, which contains personal observations, it is not about my architecture, but the way we, in our studio, think and proceed collaboratively in realising it. Architecture is not owned, it is a shared experience during the process and after it is completed. *(Ian Ritchie with Gordon Talbot, Anthony Summers, Simon Conolly, Henning Rambow, Klaus Schnetkamp, Edmund Wan, Mark Innes and Eldon Croy.)*

I would like to thank all those collaborators in Europe with whom we have had much more pleasure than pain: the clients who have entrusted us with helping them to realise their dreams and aspirations; the industries who have shared in our ideas and enabled them to materialise; the professional consultants who have motivated and enriched us; the artists who have inspired and sometimes upset us; the studio colleagues who have since moved on to develop their own careers; and personally to acknowledge Peter Rice, an irreplaceable friend, to whom I am indebted for his invitation to join him and Martin Francis in establishing, with Henry Bardsley and colleagues, the Rice Francis Ritchie design engineering studio in Paris in 1981; Peter's inspiration and humanity nurtured RFR and demonstrated the value and joy of collaborating in an atmosphere free of professional barriers; and finally, Jocelyne and Inti for those extra special pleasures of life.

Editorial Offices
42 Leinster Gardens London W2 3AN

Senior Designer: Andrea Bettella
Designer: Jan Richter
House Editor: Maggie Toy
Editor: Iona Spens

Cover: Glass circulation tower, Reina Sofia Museum of Modern Art, Madrid; *Page 2*: Bioclimatic facades, La Villette National Museum of Science, Technology, Paris

All illustrative material courtesy of the architect. The trialogue on collaboration p21 is reprinted courtesy of the Public Art Commissions Agency from *Context and Collaboration*, International Art Symposium, Birmingham, England 1990

First published in Great Britain in 1994 by
ACADEMY EDITIONS
An imprint of the Academy Group Ltd

ACADEMY GROUP LTD
42 Leinster Gardens London W2 3AN
ERNST & SOHN
Hohenzollerndamm 170, 1000 Berlin 31
Members of the VCH Publishing Group

ISBN 1 85490 294 6 (HB)
ISBN 1 85490 292 X (PB)

Distributed to the trade in the United States of America by
ST MARTIN'S PRESS
175 Fifth Avenue, New York, NY 10010

Printed and bound in Singapore

CONTENTS

INTRODUCTION

This book describes issues which concern us in the process of realising our architecture, and it is essentially in two parts. The first describes our position with regard to wider topics within which architecture takes place. The second part presents those concerns which are central to our architectural activity and illustrates how we deal with them. It does not catalogue individual projects, although aspects of our projects are used to illustrate particular issues.

Preparing an illustrated document of projects would inevitably risk submerging, through the impact of images, that which is important to us. It would also, almost inevitably, lead to a book resembling a promotional document. Thus the opportunity was taken to collect our thoughts, from the very general to the particular, to filter them together in our studio, and then to set out to provide the reader with what one might describe as a tangential text; tangential in the sense that our concerns, observations and attitudes might hopefully cause the reader frequently to pause, reflect and take off on their own trajectory.

As many of our built projects have been fairly widely published over the years in European architectural and design magazines, it seemed much more interesting to put forward the how, why and when, rather than a detailed account of what we have done in the past. In this respect the contents of the book are current and inform our present and future activities. In the future I hope to archive our past work in book form, illustrating each project as stories, capturing not only the thinking, products and final architectural objects, but also the emotional aspects involved in participation, collaboration and conflict in areas such as tactics, risks and compromise so rarely apparent in architectural publications.

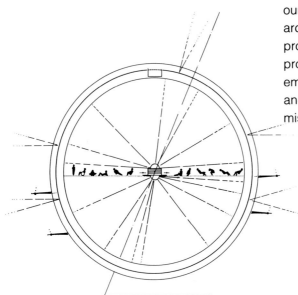

Above: Early concept diagram for the Meridian Planetarium, Greenwich;
Opposite: Structural components of the tower, Reina Sofia Museum of Modern Art, Madrid

ARCHITECTURE MEETS PLURALISM

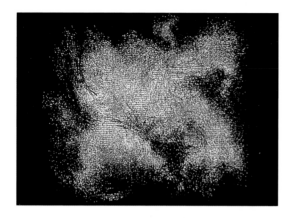

From above: Poiesis Generator; Fluy House, Picardy, France; Boulogne Harbour, France

Architecture expressing freedoms rather than equalities

Has there really been any fundamental change in architectural design since Modernism's faith in social equality based on the application of science and technology for the collective good?

Certainly the art of the late 19th century – the Impressionists, whose canvas only comes into focus when viewed from a distance, followed by the Cubists and the phenomena of abstraction, reflected the changing perception of our cosmos (order) as described by science. Quantitative rationality was being replaced by quantum theory. Has there been a significant shift in art since? The Minimalists and conceptual art of the 60s, developed from Duchamp and inspired by Cage and others reflected the period of challenge to materialism, mechanistic reason and order as social and political objectives. Architectural design did not appear to shift significantly during this period but continued to provide for a society mechanistically pursuing material ends. Art may have left behind its pre-20th-century role for society, but architecture, while inescapably tied to utility (function) and industry, appears unable to do this.

A degree of disbelief in progress based on science and technology has, in the last two decades, begun to slowly percolate through to general society; whether as a result of ecological damage awareness (largely blamed on technological progress), or because science remains a dangerous mystery to most people (still focused primarily on war machines) and is incapable of providing a decent supply of potable water.

Nevertheless, our scientific culture remains the dominant authority, even if some of its more outspoken members (Bohm, Sheldrake, Kapra, Lovelock) have seen parallels between certain aspects of the new science and non-institutionalised spirituality.

It is in this climate that a certain populist appropriation of architectural design has occurred, giving a sense of legitimate action in the face of experts (for scientist read architect). This creates for those participating both a sense of humanising science and a feeling of taking parts of their lives into their own hands – 'freedom'. However, this still leaves these actions measured against the dominant scientific cultural authority. This ambivalent position is further confounded by the fact that this public, as individuals, whilst genuinely seeking a practical say in their environment remain largely materialistic and beneficiaries of the gadgets of technology, whether medical, domestic, communications, entertainment or locomotive.

Within this populist framework falls community architecture, self-build and 'post-modern architecture', the latter finding a comfortable home within the commercialism of popular taste fabricated by Disney. They are expressions of an (aesthetic) freedom in a breathing space created as a by-product of scientific culture's own problems of coming to terms with its own loss of certainty and hence power.

So called high-tech architecture remains mainstream Modernism, a sometimes would-be specialist (scientific) neo-constructionism – served by science and technology but with little concern for equality (social concerns having become marginalised), and reflects a relationship with industry through its desire for a machine aesthetic. Latched onto by the architectural media in the early 70s as a 'style', it originated from two parallel notions: one based on recognising the constant change in society and the environment and seeking to represent this; and the second, that the means of advanced technical production had developed its own aesthetic – the dry mechanical assembly of manufactured products. The predominant interpretation of the first was to visually endorse change by suggesting that the buildings should be capable of change themselves, so fitting the second notion in which elements of the building could be unclipped, unzipped, undressed and redressed – a sort of industrial couturier architecture, temporary and therefore short-term fashion (obsolescence). The internal spatial interpretation of this adaptability created the large, often banal, open plan. These spaces were occasionally made visually seductive, but did they consider the user, or was the user in effect being asked to adapt to this sort of space by personally changing habit? The other model, less 'architectural' involved using relocatable prefabricated buildings – change with conservation, such as Cedric Price's InterAction offices.

The 'high-tech' approach embraced and promoted the notion of change, reflecting the emerging consumer society; but does it really serve it? By abdicating permanent spatial design, whether internal or external, or both, it permits the user to carry out the change; but how many 'high-tech' architects will let this happen without feeling somewhat aggrieved as 'their' building metamorphoses. The first of these notions, change, has been virtually abandoned, overlooked or forgotten, and it could even be suggested that many of these architects are no longer aware of this. Original 'high-tech' architecture was a clear rejection of the notion of permanence in a changing world, the antithesis of architectural precedence.

Deconstruction suggests that man and energy, but not power, are decentralised from the product. It alludes to the insignificance of man in relation to the planet, cosmos or multiverse. By subjugating human utility it suggests a break away from the conventional role of architecture as serving society in a practical way and hints at the first notes of challenge, in the way art did in the 60s, to our way of perceiving architecture in the present economic and political western world. Because of its controversial aesthetic, it forces architectural thinking beyond conventional boundaries of architecture. In the design of the Galleries at La Villette, by Tschumi, this decentralisation was expressed in the formal composition and through the decentring of the natural lines of force in the structure. By purposely misaligning the axial flow of energy into and through the structural joints, they appear totally over-engineered and crude because we are still dealing with solid state materials, not fluids or living organisms. Where constructivism embraced the process, the material and the technology of its age, most notably steel, the deconstructivists have yet to identify clearly the materials which best represent the decentralisation of man. The aesthetic of deconstruction is vulnerable to plagiarism devoid of meaning; while the protagonists of deconstruction battle with the pressures of utility and function.

In contrast, 'neo-historicism' alludes to classical composition while often benefiting from, yet visually subjugating contemporary industrial production. This median line of classical architecture suggests an historical authenticity to which all western architecture should align itself, and which today finds such diverse expressions in the architectural market place of styles as neo-Anglo Palladianism, neo-Greek, neo-Roman, and neo-Gothic. To the general public its formal familiarity probably gives an illusion of continuity, of permanence in the present architectural world of pluralistic styles, whether applied to the volume house builders' front door designs or office buildings.

The modernists' dream of an available architecture concerned itself principally with public housing, community health and recreation (as distinct from 'leisure' which has been turned into another commodity) and the quality of the factory environment. UK housing today is left to the 'dream homes' business with their 'tudorbethan' double garage and en suite kitchen and lounge, or the community architect as enabler when public funds are available. Is the new work place architecture of country business parks environmentally anything more than bushy car

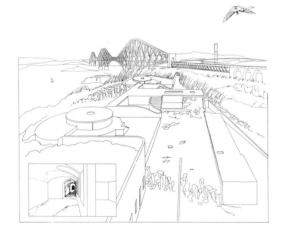

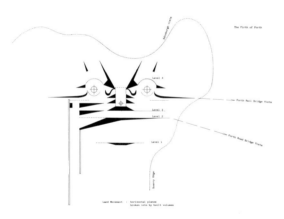

From above: Dortmund housing, Germany; Stephenson House, the
Emplacement, N Queensferry, Scotland; *Overleaf*: Marsham Street, the
Labyrinth of Political Quotations and Garden of Environmental Expression:
received words of political wisdom through history organised as a labyrinth under
the garden (quotes in stone, paper, screens, sound). Minotaur: the public exits up
the Anxiety Spiral (ASP) towards the 'real world' and the Minotaur Experience
(ME), witnessing symbols of fear and the need for man to recognise and manage
fear (technology, cultural diversity, continuous movement). The garden's one-
way glass floor area permits a discreet view of the labyrinth below, and some trees
under which to contemplate. Walking south towards the sun, the visitor chooses
one of the Resource and Information Centres of the Environment (RICE), Climate
of Complexity or the Surface of the Earth, passing or pausing in the Garden of
Environmental Expression (GEE!). Icarus: the visitor takes the escalator flight
from within either RICE centre to the glass cloud to sight London, to dream of
optimistic futures in an age of uncertainty and consider the real/unreal, natural/
artificial world of groundlessness. Come back to earth with a bump via elevators

parks with en suite fax, phone and shared toilets; the
latter separating the work place architecture from the
modern car with its telecommunications kit in the front
seat? The emerging 'hot-desking' based on the thirty to
forty per cent redundancy rate of the typical workstation
lies between the car and the present office.

With housing throughout Central Europe and the UK in
such short supply is it not time to reinvest energies in
public housing not only in terms of utility, but of a spatial
architecture that can elevate the spirit as well as answer
the economic and functional needs of a society that is
becoming more and more an urban grouping of individually minded inhabitants? Or will the market-led, con-
sumption-saturated conscience lead to a 'wallet exhibit-
ing' aesthetic for social housing too?

Certainly the pluralism of today's architecture has
placed a range of styles in front of the consumer, but
which if any of them respond to the more fundamental
issues facing society? This architectural pluralism seems
to reflect our pluralist society. More people today accept
that their own lives and society is full of contradictions,
that science does not offer solutions or indeed explain
everything. In western society there is a sense that the
private life of the individual is now far more important
than the public responsibility, which is a reversal of
general attitudes held only a few decades ago. Individuals seek other individuals with whom they have some
empathy. In a wider context political pluralism, for
example in Italy, appears to express this basic change in
society. Both at the individual level and the management
level of society, diversity will inevitably increase. We still
consider our society democratic, but our political structures have yet to adapt to this fundamental shift in
individuality, indeed no democracy has as yet embraced
men and women as genuine equals.

Architecture has to address these issues and through
challenging an urbanism of fear begin to describe
spaces which have a meaning in the sense of linking
private and public domains, in ways not solely dictated
by divisive economic preconceptions and consumerism.

Our minds, which even now are only just awakening
after years of materialism, are infected with the
despair of disbelief, of lack of purpose and ideal.
The nightmare of materialism, which has turned the
life of the universe into an evil, useless game, is not
yet past; it holds the awakening soul still in its grip.
Only a feeble light glimmers like a tiny star in a vast
gulf of darkness.
(*Kandinsky*, Concerning the Spiritual in Art, *1911*)

In the present society the quantitative and qualitative criteria for judging design can be summed up as: does it attract the consumer . . . Designers have always had more noble standards of appreciating their creations, but in practice the question of functionality, as in doing the job set out for it, of originality of design, of cultural sensitivity or of environmental impact are in this society predicated on the ultimate determining factors – does it in a direct or indirect manner generate financial wealth and/or serve to perpetuate the political and economic status quo?'

(*Pippo Lionni,* Up Against a Well-designed Wall, *Paris, 1993*)

Architecture, ecology and global economics

Ecology and global economics are inextricably linked and reflect the exploitation of energy as the source of power politically transformed into the wielding of it. Global economic history has shown this – ask any economist. We have also seen that profit from the world economy appears to shift over time around the world, as a privileged surplus (eg Medicis to the Japanese Corporations via the British Empire and the USA). We cannot continue to plunder/exploit from one part of our common home (planet) without it affecting negatively another part. A new (human) economic order is required where there is more ecological or holistic *eco*-nomic exchange as a basis for man's collective well-being and his survival.

A new wider and more appreciative Europe is hopefully not simply the creation in the coming years of the largest, most powerful single economic market that the world has ever seen, but a staging post, symbolic of a desire to achieve a more integrated whole world.

Monetary economics has so far failed to find a way of dealing with social costs or with renewable resources. The present western mania (indeed more and more global) for development based on a mechanistic and materialistic viewpoint, supported by the present inadequate economic methodology has led to increased pollution, both on a global and local scale. To most economists it appears that the social and environmental costs still remain intangible. One may think that the point of economics is to help us manage the world better, however I suspect that few economists see it this way. It seems inevitable that there must be a change in the current economic way of thinking. Man developed the present model and our actions still maintain it. A sustainable economy means a more compassionate one, in the way we relate to each other and the planet. The earth

owes man nothing. The global spread of the free market economy (so far leaving aside the polar regions) sucking the earth's wealth will probably lead our present concept of progress into oblivion. Excessive borrowing from each other and our children is wrong.

Exchange through discussion and openness of information is essential for understanding, and when this engages cultural exchange a major prerequisite for creativity is in place. This in turn makes creativity more accessible and maybe more democratic in a less competitive environment. Competition has been and remains the conceptual trigger of our present economy and society. We do not believe this is inevitable, as is often argued. Collaboration, co-operation and indeed altruism is as common a natural inheritance as 'survival of the fittest'. This is a clue to redefining economic ethics where the economy is seen not only to serve people in a material sense but involves a wider, more holistic context where non-material issues are as important as material ones.

The Information Age economy has emerged from scientific investigations and applied research of the last few decades. The time gap between science research and its exploitation is diminishing continually. The desire to respond economically is ever faster (and larger) and is leaving little time for a deeper reflection and assessment of the wider social and global value of economic decisions. This attitude has appeared even more concentrated among the English speaking countries as a result of a politic of 'deregulated individualism'.

Quantum mechanics has shown that we are not observers but participants in the world around us, and yet through our limited human perceptions we continue to describe and prescribe as if our minds were still outside our own bodies and environment. The study of ecology has brought this into focus for us. Science has also shown us that the only certainty about certainty is uncertainty. These observations which have undermined science's own imperious position ought to be making us more tolerant and more ready to participate together in many more aspects of life.

In the UK, the sense of community has been steadily eroded by state administered welfare and the politics of individualism. It is common to hear that communities only form themselves and act as such when confronted by a shared understanding of being threatened. This is largely true but reflects current society where it is evidently more difficult to achieve a sense or need of community when things appear to be going well individually. Even the City of London recharged its sense of community when threatened economically by the Canary Wharf development. Now it is reflecting again (a sort of belated pantheism) as it recognises that a bald or feathered Canary Wharf is an integral part of the 'image' of London, and that outsiders perceive London as a whole and not just as individual centres of excellence, whether financial, cultural or educational. This parochialism, with its sense of pride, endemic throughout the current 'Europe of Cities', ought to promote the significant need to understand and enjoy, at the macro and micro community scale, cultural complexity and diversity.

Is not the art of living the ultimate art? In the end, it is not the planet which is at risk but man's place (and existence) with it. Our present concern for the planet appears to be a reflection of our selfishness. We hear and talk about the loss of the world's natural resources, plant and living organisms, both in our own country and across the planet, but more often than not in the camouflaged context of our human survival through nature's diverse resource for human welfare (medical, etc).

It is important to participate as an individual to express concerns about the wider issues which affect architecture. Like holography, in each part is the whole; but unlike the hologram, each part is important to the whole. Ideas popularised in the 60s, dematerialism (conceptual art), ecological awareness, spaceship earth – world citizen and the revolution in life-styles (sexual and religious taboos) have been slowly and discreetly absorbed and transformed by western society into more practical and vociferous views on how to begin solving world issues such as hunger, pollution and inter-cultural communications. (Some would argue that this is potentially another form of colonialism.) Yet the economic model remains impervious to them.

In our urban environments, also spreading globally and 'home' to a larger and larger percentage of the earth's inhabitants, there is a danger that we are establishing an exaggerated and cocooned sense of our own self-sufficiency, which in turn will further alienate us from the essence of life on earth. This major world environmental issue was not even on the 1992 agenda of the World's first environmental conference in Rio de Janeiro.

Collectively man 'heads' starship earth and we should be taking a stronger view and measuring our actions in terms of this responsibility to all life on it. Spaceship earth will fly on regardless of whether we are comatosed or absent from the pilot's seat. The architecture we produce, and how we make our buildings, is a reflection of our world view, or 'how we walk on the earth'. This is difficult for architects to assess in real terms within a society still dominated by the science and technology culture.

Access to hard facts on energy, labour, social impact, recyclability, and the renewability of materials used in construction is very difficult. Graphs depicting comparative energy consumption of, for example, extracting raw materials or of processing them do exist. However, these 'facts', important as they are in signalling awareness, represent little in terms of the more complete picture. For example, we do not necessarily have the combined knowledge of the energy source used, the comparative polluting effects, the effect of these processes on the health of the workers in these industries and consequent social as well as economic cost etc. It is a mistake to assume that graphs or tables such as these give a whole picture. The importance and dependence on such abstracted and limited data discredits us. It is in these sorts of areas that information needs careful examination but will ultimately, one hopes, through significant development begin to give us clear data on which to make our more holistic judgements on not just materials, but the entire construction process and the way we access and use our built architecture; in fact a more whole picture of the consequences of our decisions and choices.

Another important viewpoint is the effect (visual, psychological, physiological) of the architecture on the 'user'. Healthy built environments for humans comprise one important aspect of a continuing biosphere.

Professionalism, ethics and morality

Let us not forget that architecture, as a profession, is new. It did not exist before the industrial revolution, and neither did the professions of engineering, quantity surveying, planning or many other professions which we accept as part of our everyday context. Renaissance man used the term 'architect' but not in the sense of a profession. In fact, it is recognised that the Renaissance artist (eg Piero della Francesca, Leonardo da Vinci) was often the best practising mathematician/engineer of his day.

What gave birth to the 'professionalism' of architecture? Apart from a protectionist strategy of a few elitists, to be leaders in charge, was it also a response to master the explosive shift in our cultural base; to master the nature of change, of the discovery of new materials and techniques? Certainly, the mechanised means of production dramatically changed western society and the environment, as is the information/communication revolution radically changing our present society.

Was it as a result of new materials, new techniques,

new production and assembly methods that the traditional craftsman's approach became too slow in its natural evolution to cope with the change in speed of change brought about by these inventions?

It is probable that by establishing a profession, architects had a clearer collective identity which they felt enabled them to lobby better government institutions and companies, particularly in seeking a lead role on major infrastructure projects during the second half of the 19th century.

Certainly the architect took to the 'overview role' in the same spirit as Renaissance man, and by beginning to distance the mind from the practical application, ie the trades, began a process of social hierarchy in the realisation of architecture, where mental skills combined with overview allowed the separate development of ideas, the direct discourse with clients and the establishment of the 'professional'. Over time this has led the profession of architecture to be distanced not only from industry, but also from the end user.

The education of architects reinforced this and in doing so distanced architects from others, who one by one formed their own professions of engineering, landscape, surveying and so on to the extent that today, ironically, none of the professional institutions on their own is capable of achieving a sufficiently powerful lobby to significantly influence government, one of the key

objectives identified initially as a reason to form the architectural profession. The problem now is that these institutions have become too self-centred for the benefit of the built environment as a whole, as none is capable of taking a sufficiently wide view of the many and complex issues involved. There is no justification for institutes to practise professional or educational apartheid while talking of openness – and when we all know that the process of architecture is always collaborative.

What is required at a strategic level is a Centre of Philosophy for the Environment (COPE!) which draws on the expertise from all areas of knowledge of our built and unbuilt environment. The objectives must be to raise the quality of our understanding and quality of our environmental fabric. It requires inspiration, ideas and expertise which must come not just from the 'professions' but also from artists, poets, economists and members of the public. We need to remember that currently no architectural institution provides a framework in which potential clients can learn how to be clients in relation to architects and the other professions, yet much of our built environment is commissioned by them. As institutions they administrate on behalf of their membership, but they don't really inspire anyone other than themselves.

This fragmentation at the intellectual and theoretical level – and we would include educational institutions – cannot be sustained if we are to achieve real improvements.

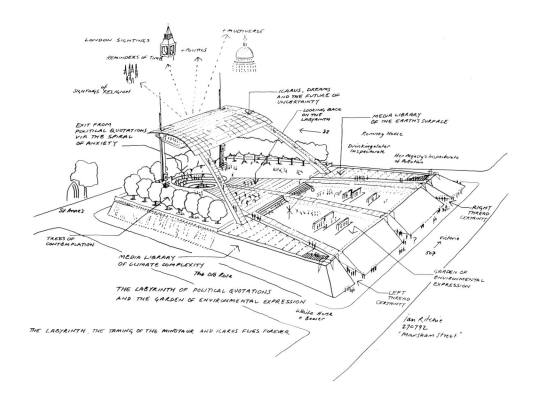

THE MEDIATISATION OF ARCHITECTURE

From above: New Meridian Planetarium, Greenwich; The Louvre pyramid, Paris (IM Pei); Ian Ritchie Architects' Studio, Wapping

Influence of the architectural press – pre-empting experience

The number of different published magazines and books on or related to architecture has increased dramatically in the UK and Europe over the last decade, and belatedly, television has now joined in the debate. Architecture has become a publicly valid culture recently through its mediatisation. This appears to reflect both the growing interest in the subject and the consequence of exploiting the accessibility and ease of publishing in this information age. Even the new Prince of Wales' Institute of Architecture in London clearly recognised this in appointing a journalist as its first director in 1992. As the quantity has increased, what of the quality? Superficially, many of the weekly, monthly and bi-monthly magazines and journals seem to carry the same 'news', buildings, products, with less and less regard for difference in the content of the article. A slight bias here and there to 'identify' journalistic originality occurs in the same way that daily newspapers slant their opinions on the same news items. This is best illustrated by the repeated publications of the same buildings not actually visited in the flesh by any representative of the magazine, hence leading to little original or total absence of critique, and often a distortion of 'reality'. Is this a cheap way of filling the publication to maintain the advertisers' revenue?

This saturation of projects, clearly reaching a lot of people creates an 'appreciation environment' which pre-empts discovery and experience of the real thing. This is most apparent amongst architectural students, who prone to strong opinions have often formed these based solely on media information. This blurring of real and artificial is very worrying. I do not want to appear elitist, recognising that the cost involved in visiting far away buildings is real, but it is leading to a dangerous situation where real experience is becoming less important, where important issues no longer appear at all in the theoretical constructs of architecture as a direct result of the media not mediatising them or deciding to filter them out.

This recalls the story in the early years of cinematography when a Chicago gang in the first decade of this century used a large cumbersome camera set-up to rob jewellers shops. Onlookers, fascinated, even ten years or so after the public became familiar with films, believed that the 'smash and grab' was only being acted for film.

Today, developments in virtual reality are producing technological products which may have significant value in certain situations (eg medicine). They are certainly going to be popularised by the manufacturers, which will create yet another more exotic avenue out of reality. Is reality really so bad? Or are we gradually metamorphosing mammals whose artificial stimuli will be plugged directly into our synapses?

Exploiting the press: cheap publishing and propaganda
One can only conclude that the purpose of this increasing phenomenon of a 'personality culture' in architectural publications is primarily to massage egos, both of architects and industry seeking publication for 'kudos' or for free advertising or for 'training' young journalists. What one does not fully understand yet is why so much of it appears? We can appreciate that with one decent computer and software pack, a link to an electronic publisher, publishing is economically accessible and could become a valuable source of employment – but this doesn't have to lead to such superficial and narrowly focused contents. This again reflects a society besotted with 'information' and with consumption, without moving towards an intelligent use of information.

The media generally has focused its attention too much on surface style, and in the process has 'grouped' architects by style. In the first half of this century, architects, particularly Europeans, were involved in written debates and manifestos about the social promise of architecture and the process of building. The current preoccupation with image (consumerism), rather than content (utility), has consequently swept aside this sociopolitical concern, which says as much about architects today as it does about the media.

It also suggests that the quantity of information produced today has created a 'bytes battlefield'. In this information theatre, where the typical patient has a limited attention span and picture bytes are more penetrative than the printed word (hence TV interest), the future for more serious discussion will probably remain on the margins, in the form of academic papers prepared at universities.

Appearing on TV or participating in a radio programme discussing architecture demands pre-planning; eg, for a recorded programme – to go for the sixty to ninety-second solo performance with a construct which makes it almost impossible for one's contribution to be edited.

Without doubt even the more sophisticated publications depend for identity on strong visual material, which in turn places even more importance on graphic and visual content at the expense of architectural content.

This, originally sourced from new architectural graphics has led to a merging of visual architecture and art at this level, while few publications search for the architectural meaning behind this representational material.

The inevitability of individualisation and architectural heroes
From the moment institutes controlling professions established themselves, the architect, whose authorship of design was vested in him, reinforced his position as originator-leader and controller of the project. Inevitably, although some 150 years since the founding of many 'institutes of architects', this 'authorship' has led inexorably to the media cultivation of the architectural hero.

The practice of architecture is not individual, despite the emphasis still placed on it in most schools of architecture. Architectural achievement is a result of bringing out the best through collaboration. Architecture can in a sense be promiscuous; fine arts, for example seeking the loose edges of architecture for collaboration while allowing the artist to remain individualistic. Does identity of an idea need to remain and be recognised as originating from a particular person in our office? No, but generally it does take time for this to be overcome amongst new graduates. The social structure of our open office is based on the entire staff, with individual projects generally supported by a maximum of five staff. It is not possible for selfish egos to survive in the atmosphere created by this arrangement. This structure and atmosphere 'breaks down the apparently hierarchic structure into one in which it is clear where authority lies and yet where all feel able to (freely) contribute and generate ideas'. (From *Design in Mind* by Professor Bryan Lawson on Ian Ritchie)

The fact that individuals do express themselves within this clear context reinforces both the individual as indispensable and creative, and the quality of the collaborative effort. It is almost as if in our studio overlooking the Thames and the wide horizons of south London we have managed to create a pocket of harmony and respect for each other.

Participation should draw people together and result in more awareness and knowledge of others. Survival instincts do not require us to know the inner or outer secrets of individuals. We think everybody in this age is trying to develop, and in this sense it is vital to recognise everyone's hunger for creativity and expression and that individuals will always seek out those things to which they can relate for their own benefit. It is this, which through the mediatisation of the individual hero, seduces and ultimately distorts the relationship of individual benefit to creative development in a participatory context.

The stillness of silent communication through our work and not ourselves makes it difficult to mediatise us as a group or as individuals. All creative people, artists and clients have a common need to research and develop ideas privately and all recognise that this work must eventually be made public – presented by them. The publication of this work can help sustain their existence, and by implication they all inevitably depend to some extent on the media.

There is no doubt in my mind that the 80s almost deified the individual and his greed in a free market economy, and that the burgeoning architectural press went with this tide. More recently, a few architectural publishers are reflecting and contributing positively to the debate on society as a whole which is seeking sustainable new directions.

The myth of the individual is created and nurtured by a bland human curiosity through an exploitative and propagandist media.

It is said that we all have need of heroes,
but then heroes become fashion,
and fashion can lead to fascism.
Maybe the tide of the individual is now on the ebb,
thank goodness.

Il n y a point de héros pour son valet de chambre: 'No man is a hero to his valet.' (*Mme Cornuel*)

Andrea: Unhappy the land that has no heroes.
Galileo: No, unhappy the land that needs heroes.
(*Berthold Brecht*, Leben de Galilei)

Smokescreens, populism and the avant-garde

Much has been said and written on the failures of Modernism, and many descriptions of Post-Modernism have been proffered, without consensus or conclusion. It has often been argued that PoMo originated in architectural works (post Venturi's Las Vegas). Maybe the visual arts adopted PoMo through rejection of the abstraction of Modernism rather than creation, or through adoption of seemingly unsophisticated popular expressions. The transfer of these visuals onto architecture, in a manner not unlike the transfer of technological images of high-tech, reflected society's preoccupation with the superficial.

In essence, symmetry is at the root of classical architectural composition, while asymmetry characterised much early avant-garde architecture, abstract and concrete painting, sculpture and music. Abstraction and asymmetry were, and to a large extent remain, alien to popular taste. Some seventy years on, the resurrection of popular taste (ie recognisable/acceptable) in architec-

ture has seen two generic typologies – PoMo pastiche (disneyesque) and neo-neo-classical. The former resurrects historical elements (pre-19th century) whose confection whether applied in large or small amounts aims to popularise. The latter attempts to restate the 'one true' language of architecture. Both demonstrate a massive loss of faith in the present and future. Both have managed, however, to put the brakes on modern architecture's desire to reflect its own age, producing a smoke screen behind which time has become available. This has given some architects the opportunity to reassess the values of Modernism in contemporary society.

Unfortunately western society has not generally been interested in the rethinking of architecture as a social tool, but rather as a fashionable or wallet-flashing product (ie, value rather than utility). If it had represented more, then Modernism's concerns with political and social objectives would have succumbed to more questioning, development and new directions. Where Modernism helped define and identify through its architecture the emerging middle class, today, through manipulation by the media culture, the middle classes are seen to be defining modernity and its architecture.

Modern architecture's apparent marriage to science, and its arguments of reason, logic, methodology, honesty and rationality of fact, continues despite the fact that science has and remains conjectural at any given time. Science has always discreetly allowed space for new ideas while often appearing dogmatic. Today, more and more people understand that science is gently shedding its historical dogmatism and it is into this space that New Age and Post-Modern movements have found the opportunity to enjoy mediatisation. Modernism has not died, but is redefining itself more loosely as Modernity. Only political monetarism, applying itself globally, appears relentless in its self-belief and authority. Modernism (form follows function) and the avant-garde Post-Modernism (function follows form) are both singular, and in arguing their own singular legitimacy are denying the fact that all rules have their own boundaries.

There is no universal rationality. This questions the validity of any one holistic theory of architecture at any one time. What do exist within a moral context are ideas responding to needs and perceived challenges. It is the subjectivity of perception and the moral position of those who create which produces the diversity characteristic of today's architecture.

Experiments in spatial form are not testing any architectural theory but are attempting to break new ground in

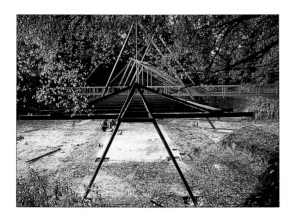

spatial perception to satisfy desire. The more extreme they are the more they are seen as avant-garde. What is clear is that it is the 'aesthetic' of avant-garde architecture in much the same way as the avant-garde aesthetic in music which is controversial ('silence'– Cage) and sometimes subversive (and by implication political).

It is also necessary to release, often only temporarily, culture from its big sleep of habit, inertia and automatism which commerce exploits in the form of mass consumption. In music, cultural development rather than routine over the past quarter of a century has shown how unpopular rock, punk, house, deep house tech, even pop and 'concrete music' were when they began. They did not seek popularity, but a need to satisfy creative desires, and once popular they are then denied or treated condescendingly by the culturally 'aloof'. They see it as intellectually void, and that which they endorse is dismissed largely by the populist culture because of its intellectual labelling. Popular culture conveys little about its values to society other than that the originators of these various forms of expression were often anything but popular, and that today that which is initially unpopular is a major source of material for the exploitative mass consumer juggernaut.

From above: House at Eagle Rock, Sussex under construction; Pharmacy, Boves, France

CHANGE

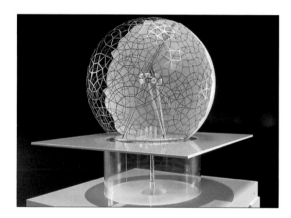

From above: Poiesis Generator (computer simulation graphics, Olivier Auber); Model of Pearl of the Gulf, Dubai; Light installation, Ingolstadt

Change in the rate of change

The medium of change is communication. The rate of change results directly from the speed of communication. The change in the rate of change during the latter part of the 20th century has been a crucial factor in making people feel ambivalent towards progress. During the past two electron decades, time and space boundaries to communication have disappeared and transmission and reception are now virtually simultaneous.

With the information that is now available to us there is a need to assess the real value of this information and to understand how best to use it. Information is either mind generated or mind filtered. At the moment those in powerful positions of access and ability to manipulate large quantities of information, to process and distribute it at great speed, reflect a society reluctant to change its use of information other than as the major fuel of the current global economy.

The balance between individual well-being and the future direction of society depends on recognising that today's electronic communication has created such an awareness of global interdependence that all actions and reactions should have a moral base. It will become increasingly difficult to ignore cause and effect consequences of individual and corporate actions which, hopefully, will increase social accountability. We should be looking towards an Age of Intelligence, both human and cybernetic, where morality informed by cultural and environmental awareness is concerned with both global and local welfare.

Those who have knowledge and those who are creating it are both continuing to expand. It will surely follow that thought and action will increase in complexity, diversity and speed, and much of it will be increasingly communicated 'screen to screen' (neuron to neuron) than eyeball to eyeball. What has been the effect of electronic speed on architecture?

Recognising that the design of space and light in architecture has always had the opportunity to respond to the latest technologies, there is little doubt that material research and building assembly techniques are developing new horizons at an ever increasing rate thanks to the electronic speed of information handling and communication, and increasingly between machines.

Architectures are now imagined on screens in space time, as are geometries at the limits and beyond human drafting abilities. Whole architectural compositions are transmitted to remote clients and industry for approval and realisation even to the extent of avoiding direct emotional contact. We have already completed a project in France solely using telecommunications and we have seen how to eliminate traditional shop drawing/fabrication procedures by direct data transfer to computer controlled machines in the fabrication works. We are also aware of the research and progress that is being made in site construction robotics (noting that worldwide sales in robotics apparently peaked in 1987!). We have experienced that the quantity of information that can be handled and its speed of communication can release even more creativity and the time within which to be creative. However, the time made available can also be eroded by the administration, filtering and misapplication of computer processed information, and also the belief of some clients and contractors that project design periods can be shortened ('fast track construction-fast track design'), which ignores and misunderstands the essential time for reflection and gestation of ideas.

By the end of the 1960s the electronic age had arrived and was instrumental in the formulation of projections on the nature of future society, many of which gained 'credibility'. These included a leisure society whose people would be largely working from home, a thirty-hour working week, retiring at forty and relaxing through a 'second life'. At the increasingly computerised banks, home banking and shopping were seen as natural adjuncts to a home based life and there were forecasts of a cashless society. Thirty years on, the gregarious nature of man, his continued love affair with the automobile, his attachment to cash and the collapse of the 'traditional family unit' are some of the characteristics which have left these 60s projections well and truly beached. Employment and under-employment are not associated with the electronic age or blamed on computerisation or robotics, and those who have work are hanging on to it and working just as many hours, if not more, rather than looking or hoping for early retirement. And the paper offices, rather than disappearing as was often forecast, have big notices to recycle paper: 'hard copy still rules'. So it would appear evidently foolish to predict society's future, but interestingly not without reason to suggest technical advances and new developments which will in some way or another have a significant impact on it.

Directions of change
The next major acceleration in the rate of change has begun with the first photonic computer prototypes. Good night electron, the Photonic Age is here!

The inevitability of lighter and smaller hardware, faster processing and transmission based on the speed of light (currently our only real speed limit!) will be the basis for this acceleration.

Light-weight space telecommunications packages with holographic memory banks will be launched in the near future by photon beams as the weight of these individual packages drops to a few grammes, increasing the quantity, if not the quality of internationally available information.

More and more information will flow, managed by ever more sophisticated software, and we will be drawn into a world where we can appreciate, if we so desire, a fuller interactive, animated picture from a multitude of viewpoints virtually simultaneously. The Cubists having destroyed the accepted single point of view and dynamic fractals simultaneously 'visualising' some of nature's infinite patterns, are making obsolete our trained architectural prejudice for the single viewpoint.

Equally, our non-visual appreciation of the world in which our architecture is constructed will benefit from a more holistic appreciation of the context in which we operate. We could be more efficient with resources, more responsible with materials and more considerate of building occupants' short and long term needs.

Our objective is an architecture which uses less material and that the materials used will perform better, not only technically and environmentally but also aesthetically.

As new structures and architectures developed from new materials, so too will the materials of our immediate future release us more and more from the bondage of static buildings.

COLLABORATION

From above: Concept for Digbeth Media Quarter, Birmingham; Tidal Clock, Cardiff, represented as a copper clad figurehead; Geology Museum, London

Barriers – professional

Psychological barriers occur only in the minds of men, and like any theory constructed by man these barriers can be deconstructed and replaced. In the case of 'barrier absence' this requires a way of thinking and attitude which is no longer territorial because there is respect and trust, which encourages confidence with humility between people. Professionals should be as capable of realising this as anyone else, and in terms of their influence on society and the physical environment should have a moral obligation to do so.

I know from my own experience with Peter Rice and Martin Francis, and the way our office in London functions, that territories do not have boundaries, they are simply different landscapes which require different skills to negotiate well, but also through which with one's collaborators one can be supported and supportive.

How we collaborate

In a practice which has at various times included engineer, naval architect, artist, anthropologist, photographer, landscape architect, poet, where none are regarded as technicians or draughting people, we are accustomed to the absence of barriers as we are to the absence of hierarchy. Since a small office cannot always sustain this diversity, we frequently collaborate with other professions in the usual way. It is important to do this with people who share the same objectives – for example design quality and similar values. Thus we have over the years established working relationships with a select number of consultants (whose names appear in the acknowledgements). An interesting process of mutual education and reorientation occurs when a job comes to us with another consultant already attached to it by the client, and the consequent 'heat' necessary to melt the engineering and architectural boundaries.

The kernel of creative collaboration contains several crucial ingredients:
– Each must take time to listen to the other and suspend prejudices. This not only allows mutual respect to grow, but without it the synergy of mutual creativity cannot flourish: the process like brainstorming in which nobody can quite remember where the solution came from.
– The commonality of aims is usefully complemented by a diversity of expertise.
– No barriers = no defences. There are those who feel threatened when another profession speaks their language and questions their assumption. (It is a shame we have these languages and hide behind them at times.)

This is inhibiting to any free exchange.

These principles of collaboration apply at all stages of a project; initially with a client and later with a builder or fabricator. Differences of orientation can generate conflict, or can be harnessed creatively. The trick to helping this process move in a constructive direction is often found by sticking rigorously to an open-minded approach where everyone's preconceptions – especially our own – are questioned, and we demonstrate a willingness to receive other's ideas and modify our own, whilst at the same time refusing to compromise our design principles and values. Those ideas that survive this process of challenge are stronger for having stood up to scrutiny, and the process is exciting.

> After all, we all agree on that (collaboration) . . . But talking about it doesn't seem to have had much effect. One must somehow create the conditions which will allow such collaboration to take place, and one must educate members of the building team to see their own contribution not as an end in itself, but as a part of a common endeavour to create comprehensive, total architecture.

(*Ove Arup*, Institute of Civil Engineers, 26 October 1972)

Collaborating

A dramatised discourse on collaboration between Kathryn Gustafson (landscape artist), Pippo Lionni (designer) and Ian Ritchie at the International Public Art Symposium, Birmingham, April 1990.

Gustafson [*in her studio on the telephone*]: Vivien, hi, how are you doing? What's up? I got your letter from Birmingham. What are you up to? . . . A what? . . . Yes, on what? Collaboration? What about it? . . . How to do it? Go on Vivien, it's easy. You just sit down and you start working. Maybe people aren't so successful with it, huh? . . . Yes, well I'll try.

Can I work with the guys I like to work with? . . . OK. Listen, I'll call you back. Let me talk to them. We'll see what they say, OK. Bye.

[*On phone*]

– Hey, Pippo, it's me . . . Yes, what's up? . . . These people in England, they want to know how we work. You want to try to talk about it? . . . Yes I'm serious; they want to know how we work. What do you think, why don't you come over? Have lunch or something, and talk about it.

[*Enter Lionni with suitcase*]

Lionni: Hey, how are you doing? What do they want to do?

Gustafson: They want to know how we work.

Lionni: It's not easy, you sure you want to get involved in this?

Gustafson: I know these guys, they'll pay the hotel, and you know what, £100. [*Laughter*]

Lionni: Great! Where's Ian? I haven't seen him since we worked with that jerk Kretchman back in '85 on the project for Seville. Let's get Ian in, he's great. He's respectable.

Gustafson: You think he's presentable?

Lionni: Yeah, he's presentable. He doesn't have much time. Call him up.

Gustafson: He's hot now, you know that?
   [*On phone*] – Is Ian Ritchie there? Kathryn Gustafson speaking . . . yes . . . [*aside*] real serious, he's a big time architect, eh?

Lionni: I hope he comes in a suit, tell him to bring a suit.

Gustafson: He hates suits.
– Ian, it's Kathryn, how are you? . . . No, no it's OK.

Lionni: Collaboration, wow! And in a suit.

Gustafson: Would you stop talking, I'm trying to talk on the phone.
– Ian, listen these people in Birmingham. You know Birmingham? . . . yeah.

Lionni: He knows Birmingham!

Gustafson: He knows Birmingham.

Lionni: Wow!

Gustafson: They want us to talk about collaboration.

Lionni [*aside*]: Is that in Holland?

Gustafson: No, no, no. Pippo's across the table. We'll do it all three of us. OK . . . Yeah. We'll just get on a flight.

There's one at 11 o'clock. You'll be here in time for lunch. Use that super pass card you used to jump over the turnstiles the time we were over with Air France, you know. OK see you in a bit. You are coming? . . . OK bye.

[*Ritchie enters with travel bag*]

Lionni: Wow, look at that suit!

Gustafson: Wait a minute, wait a minute, I've got to get the food going.

Lionni: Better turn the light on.

Gustafson [*to Ritchie*]: Listen, do you want your phone calls screened? Should I just tell them you're not here any more?

Ritchie: Not here.

Gustafson: OK.

Lionni: Have you seen this picture of my kid, Luca?

Ritchie: I didn't know you were a dad.

Gustafson: Isn't he cute.

Lionni: Yeah it's great. Well, there's this thing about collaboration. The problem is it seems so damn simple.

Gustafson: But, I don't know.

Lionni: How would you start talking about it?

Gustafson: The concept.

Ritchie: Where is it?

Gustafson: No, no. What?

Ritchie: No, where is it? Collaborating with who on what? I've got lag – you know, jet lag.

Gustafson: Huh, you're only an hour away.

Lionni: You know what you should really say. The first thing is that you have to start from the beginning. You know it's not something that happens afterwards.

Gustafson [*to Lionni*]: He hasn't understood the context yet.

Lionni: We've got to talk about collaboration. We have to decide how to talk about it I guess. The first thing we should say is that we do it!

Ritchie: OK.

Lionni: And that this is it.

Ritchie: How do you do it?

Lionni: Well. You, eh . . .

Ritchie: No, you can tell me.

Lionni: Before we start I have to give these folks a little side information. [*Starts rolling out a toilet roll*]

I brought with me a special tool we use in collaboration. It's a very important tool because it's important to remember that what you do is not precious, right, and you can throw it away afterwards.

A basic point is that, for us, real collaboration started with the introduction of the 'concept' in design. That idea that brings us together; that we create together. To make the concept the first thing we do is . . . [*Rolling out toilet rolls*]

Ritchie: Hang on, hang on.

Gustafson: Do you need some help with the concept?

Lionni: I'm not there yet. The first part is about the problem.

Ritchie: Ah, the problem.

Gustafson: The problem.

Lionni: I was about to tell them OK.
[*Walking over toilet rolls*]
So the first thing you do is figure out what the problem is. It's very rare that the problem as given and the problem as understood are identical.

Gustafson: Don't walk on the problem!

Lionni: So the first thing is the problem. I want to give you an example. At this conference the problem may be 'how to incorporate art into urban or architectural projects through collaboration'. We would take that, turn it upside down and say how to do projects and design things so that they work and maybe the world changes, and we should include a lot of different people. Oh! It's hard to talk and roll out the concept at the same time.

Gustafson: I think you need help with this concept. [*Laughter*]

Lionni: So really the concept is an idea that takes into account all these problems around all these eccentric folks who come together, architects, designers, artists. [*Aside while rolling out toilet roll again*]
Don't touch my floor! [*Laughter*]
I have to throw this bit away now.
How do you work around this thing? Do you build buildings and then you put art into them?
But really you have to come together at the beginning. You have this other stage which to use the Italian term is the *progettazione* which means the act of visualising the idea; you draw it!
So what happens if at the beginning you have a concept and then in the middle you find out it wasn't the right concept at all?
[*Screws up toilet roll and throws it away*]
You have to formulate another one. You have to adapt it to the situation and there's always that real work, and then these things get tied together. Now what we do is we come together with these books [*each has a book*], we talk, we draw and keep criticising what we're doing.
You have your main idea, [*gesticulates towards toilet roll*] this is it, and afterwards you keep at it and you come back together again to verify things at this last stage. I usually come out of the picture 'cos it gets too difficult and I don't know what to do, and I hate sitting around drawing and hassling over the details.
This stage is where you build the damn thing. That's enough of that so let's talk about how you do it. OK. We'll keep this [toilet roll] handy in case we need it.

Ritchie: What you've got there is a bit of energy at the front end and that energy has to carry you through all the hassle that follows. It might be three months, it might be three years, but what you've got to get is the energy into the idea at the beginning.
Let me come back to the problem of this conference. How do you collaborate? Who, who are you?

Lionni: That's what we wanted to talk about.

Ritchie: Who you collaborate with.

Gustafson: There are some rules to that. First, choose well your partner. One of the rules about choosing your partner is respect.

Lionni: There are very few people that you can work with.

Gustafson: When you find them, hold onto them.

Lionni: It can get really hot and it's almost like love.

Ritchie: It is?

Lionni: It's love!

Ritchie: What we're trying to communicate is the way we collaborate, up front, right at the beginning. We don't use cheque books, all that stuff, money, comes out and will happen. But for the moment we have to be generous, take all these funny hats off with funny labels.

Lionni: You have to be equal and there are terrible power struggles and financial struggles in the beginning.

Gustafson: Not if you start out right. That's part of choosing partners. Someone whose mind you like and they like your mind and they're willing to listen to you. I get high thinking about your mind, that's what it's like. [*Laughter*]

Lionni: This kind of collaboration is the most incredible high that I've had in my work. What comes out of it is much, much better than any of us would do separately. When you really work together, unlike when you just bring someone in just to do a job, this gets to be something that's totally new and totally different.

Gustafson: . . . And you can't define any longer who did what on a project.

Lionni: You don't deny who you are but you leave aside any structure in order to work on it.

Ritchie: We have beside us suitcases marked architect, designer, engineer, but the skills come out naturally because of the way you work.

Gustafson: When you're choosing your partner, do you have to come from the same culture? There's one thing that's hard to define, you have to have the same abstract pattern of thoughts. You've got to figure out if you can think with the person you're going to work with.

Ritchie [*to Gustafson*]: You're an American/Scandinavian and [*to Lionni*] you're something else.

Lionni: Don't let's go into it.

Ritchie: I am a Scotsman so we do have problems at a cultural level.

Lionni: Do you remember when Peter Rice fell asleep at the table?

Ritchie: And you were ten minutes behind him.
It's about taking risks and you like working with people who like risk-taking.

Lionni: It's true, you have to put everything on the line.
Going back to the concept, you go away and do your thing, maybe strawberry shortcake, or reading books on chaos or Adorno, and you come back and say that you've got this great idea. But you've got to respect the separate time and the time when you are together, in other words you can't always sit there at the table, because you fall asleep.

Ritchie: But there's one other person.

Gustafson: You're getting out of order again, we're supposed to define who and you're into what already.

Ritchie: There's another who: that's the person who made the phone call in the first place – the client. Is she going to collaborate or is she going to be out there?

Lionni: It would really be ideal if she could come and collaborate also because collaboration between specialists leaves out the real problem. We have to collaborate in society, we have to collaborate with the client.
You haven't talked to them about the banker yet.

Gustafson: Wait a minute, try and finish with the client before we deal with the banker.

Ritchie: When I work I like the client to be part of the process. But I don't need her for the concept but you've got to tell the client you're collaborating.

Lionni: Does it or doesn't it cost more to collaborate?

Ritchie: It doesn't cost any more.

Lionni: Are you sure?

Ritchie: I don't think it costs any more but if you tell the client you're collaborating she might think it will cost her more, therefore she might find some money anyway. You leave it up to her, she's party to it. Perhaps she feels generous like we're being generous with each other.

Lionni: In France it's different because most big jobs are competitions and we are paid very little, so we always have this hassle over how to bring other folks in and not pay them, or just a little bit, like your ideas are groovy but there's really no money unless we win.

Gustafson: There is still no money. [*Laughter*]

Lionni: So you should really do it as a cause.

Ritchie: So the project becomes the most important thing, not us collaborating.

Lionni: That's the most important thing. What happens when that idea I put on the table that I've been thinking about in my dreams all night is the most beautiful and original idea I've ever had in my whole life and then everyone throws it away! You have got to decide together that this other thing we're producing, that we can't really seem to define, is more important than that idea.

Ritchie: So you've really got to keep your ego to the outside. Now is that so much?

Lionni: That's difficult!

Ritchie: Because when we get friction they're the ideas. One of the things about trying to agree, do you agree by mediocrity or do you agree because it's intense? If you don't agree, you have a problem. One of the ways of solving that is to actually move it outside so that the project is political, it's why you're actually collaborating so it diffuses and is a means to solve some of those internal frictions.

Gustafson: I still haven't finished with the client. There are some that are already educated, like at Parc de La Villette, who decided that we should collaborate; François Barré, he was incredible. I learned more from that client than I did from a lot of people.

Lionni: It's incredible, sometimes you can learn from the clients.

Gustafson: It's amazing.

Ritchie: Yeah. [*Laughter*] But what's amazing is when they've worked out that those three people actually like each other therefore we [*the client*] can tell them to collaborate. It's not the same when the client says, you, you and you, and you've never met. It's actually quite a perceptive client that sniffs you out.

Lionni: Conceptual design is really a lot about trying to educate the client. When you come back to the problem you have to talk (to the client) and tell them that the solution they've already got in mind is the solution to the wrong problem. You end up having to change that a lot.

Gustafson: Another thing that happens is that they think collaboration happens in stages instead of from the very beginning, collaborators' polka dots of art that go into buildings are not real collaboration. That line over there [*points to toilet roll*] happens in the beginning with everybody at the same time. To convince the client, you have to amass all those people right away.

Ritchie: I remember that big competition in Dubai for a monument where the client got 400 entries and he didn't like any of them. He has 400 models which he didn't like. So what did they do but ring the French Embassy for advice. They wanted an answer from the French Embassy and the French Embassy rang an artist!

Gustafson: What for?

Ritchie: Well the French thought that an artist would have the answer.

Gustafson: Did he?

Ritchie: Well it's very interesting because this artist rang me up. Now I didn't have the answer and neither did he.

Lionni: That's because he didn't want to do that last part.

Ritchie: You reckon? What was interesting though, was that they didn't get a monument, they got a symbol; they got a museum, a brand new museum. Now that client actually didn't need a symbol or a monument, what he wanted was a statement about culture.

All: So we're back to the concept (*the problem*).

Ritchie: The artist, through the freedom of exchange, enabled the thing to be redefined.

Lionni: You're still not going to talk about the banker, are you?

Ritchie: The bankers.

Lionni: Let's talk about real collaboration.

Ritchie: Like most of these things, you leap in and it's going to cost you money somewhere down the line. So you tell the client you're going to collaborate. You also tell your banker and the banker's going to raise all those other questions like financial and professional liability. Does your partner have any? And you say, hang on, this is collaboration. You then have to sit down with your banker and explain collaboration and the level of risk that's involved. You invite him in as well as the client.

Gustafson: Another thing is telling your banker that you're doing this for the public (*sector*) and the public pays six months to a year down the line, and convincing your banker that it's worth waiting for.

Lionni: I was going to talk about the rules.

Gustafson: We haven't talked about how.

Lionni: We talked about how we get together.

Gustafson: Using words is easy. When you start drawing you can't believe how many people misunderstood what you thought you said and you've misunderstood what they thought they said and they don't like what you draw and you don't like their style. What then?

Lionni: You have to know if you have the same kind of visual interpretation of these abstract ideas. There are some very important affinities that have to be there.

Gustafson: What do you do if you get halfway through a project and the client's waiting for a result within fifteen days and all of a sudden it's not working?

Lionni: That's Ian's great principle. If you can pick up that it's not going to work fast enough, it can save a lot of hassle to get out and call up another architect or someone that you know and give it to them.

Ritchie: That goes back to the triangle of confidence, the client, the industry and the collaborators, and you have this line called confidence that if it shakes a bit get ready to mend or run. If one of them goes, quit, because you won't do anything worthwhile.

Lionni: Or is it better to just do it alone?
   I'd like to talk about our commandments of collaboration:
• There has to be a moral commitment
• You have to have no preconceived idea and be open to almost anything
• You really have to listen and you have to interrupt, and be ready to be interrupted
• The ideas you have are shared: no one can claim them afterwards
• We're not competing with each other, we're just trying to make something new
• There is time together, synthetic time, and then there is reflective time when we work apart
• Each situation is unique
• The relationship is about contact
• There should be defined rules
• The participants are to be equal, there are no bosses
• You must respect the common concept as being more important than what you could have conceived by yourself
• The last and most important thing is that it's about improvisation, and that's what we did today!

DISCUSSION

From the floor: You didn't talk about the public, aren't they involved at all?

Ritchie: All of our work is public. What we are talking about is the person between the public and the client (that's usually us) and being part of the process. When we work together and collaborate, the question of friction which always arises – whether it's over the money, the design, the ethic, the morals – in the end the project is the mediator which helps to solve some of those frictions. It is also the responsibility of the public to have intermediaries that look out for their needs.

From the floor: Isn't it the responsibility of the artist as intermediary to the public?

Lionni: It's all our responsibilities.

From the floor: Can you answer the question, how do you collaborate with the public?

Gustafson: A lot of times collaborations can take several types of forms; I've been in a situation where I've worked on housing projects, rehabilitation projects for ghettos. The public sits there and yells 'We want this', etc and then a guy got up and said 'Wait a minute, I'm a plumber, I work nine hours a day being a plumber – you guys do art, landscape architecture, would you just do it!'

Ritchie: There's no formula, no panacea for working with the public, you can do it by living and working in your area for fifteen years, and just be alive.

Lionni: What we talked about today was a methodology, a way of working and I think the world of tomorrow will have problems that are more complex; designers, architects and artists will have to find new ways of solving them. We'll all have to learn new kinds of methodologies to solve problems, some of them without artists. All we did was to try to show you a kind of methodology, a way of working which can incorporate different kinds of people.
   The idea is the first and most important thing. It is a position which might be common to all three of us, and consumer responsibility and ownership the prerequisites for working together.
   This work is political in the ultimate sense. We're trying to produce a world in a little itsy bitsy way that is better to live in, where people understand more, where people are less oppressed and people live less dreary lives, where they have more control over their environment: this is the glue that brings us together.

From the floor: You have talked about your collaborative process of working together. Are you a partnership now? Do you enter competitions together?

Lionni: That brings up an important point – there is a

delicate moment when you get the phone call. For example, 'Ian Ritchie, we've got this project' – and he has to decide very quickly, as we all do, who to work with.

Ritchie: I think there's a difference when the person gets the phone call, that person makes up their mind but they also have some obligation as soon as they set up this wheel of collaboration, to inform the client. The other issues, do you have a contract between each of you, do you end up forming a company? There are other situations – I spent eight or nine years working with Martin Francis and Peter Rice. We have no written contract between us and yet we've done lots of work for central government. In other situations a contract is imposed.

Gustafson: It's very important to talk about the contract between collaborators at the beginning. Whether it's moral, verbal, define them well – where's the money going? Who puts ideas down on paper? – All of these things need to be defined.

Ritchie: In the end it's the same for all of us involved in the environment – you're faced with a problem and you come up with a concept that will become a product at the other end. In order to live with that product you attempt to do it the best way that you can.

Lionni: Also some of the best concepts have come from people who are not designers.

From the floor: I was about to make that point, we're all talking about improving the quality of the human environment. It might be creating a new environment, new form, new building, whatever, or amending existing environments. We should remember that a lot of professions affect where we live: geographers, urban planners, archaeologists and anthropologists. These people understand how environments work as well as architects and artists. Who affects the collaboration is infinite.

Lionni: It's a really complicated concept because if you go back, collaboration doesn't really mean anything and has to be defined. In any reasonable office, we collaborate with people, they are equally as important. We collaborate with people all the way down the line and it's a central part of our work.

From the floor: I can't understand why you talk about problems all the time.

Ritchie: We're not talking about solving problems. When someone rings you up and says we'd like to have a very tall ladder to get from here to there please – that's the problem that's given. When you collaborate you question the problem that's given; you question everything, you have no preconceptions at all. For example, here I made the mistake of having preconceptions – I thought of just showing slides, Kathryn and Pippo would do the same. But no we collaborated . . .

Limits of democracy: convergence out of necessity
We enjoy collaborating on projects, but it is selective. We realise that genuine collaboration is an absolute prerequisite to a successful relationship with the client.

In cities, the general public and in particular their citizens are rarely considered and treated with respect as are real user clients, but merely as passive recipients. This was made expressly evident during the 1980s when the deregulated planning and the myopic market-led development dogma of the British government crash landed in many areas of the inner city, leaving the citizen completely ignorant and ignored.

To some extent the public's profound distrust of this process was exacerbated by their loss of confidence in the democratic accountability of their elected local authorities, who behaving in a paternalistic or remote manner were treating the citizen simply as a consumer of their decisions. Equally, those architects and planners involved were seen to be inaccessible and unaccountable to the citizen.

Autonomy and collaboration are not mutually exclusive characteristics of man or societies. Self-determination is a capacity and right crucial to the psychological well-being of individuals and communities. Whether it is exercised depends on whether it is relinquished for the 'comfort' of conformity. Of course individuals and groups can be subjugated by force, whether economic, legislative or physical, but this merely confirms the existence of an external power. When this power is expressed dogmatically, as if it represents the only viable objective reality or option – and it results in failure, accountability is camouflaged behind arguments of objectivity. There is remarkable consistency for deflecting blame by those whose position, elected or otherwise, defines their actions as those of a 'servant or instrument' through which reality expresses itself. This would be much more acceptable if the reality was one which engaged, on a much more equal and sensible level, the citizens on behalf of whom decisions are supposedly taken, particularly at the local level within cities. This engagement of the citizen is often thwarted by lack of resources available to them. Voluntary commitment is often the only means to participate and this can have significant effects on social and private life.

Architecture is often quoted as being a reflection of our society, or that society deserves the architecture which is built. During the last decade, in the UK particularly, the scale and design of commercial buildings constructed in town centres and the lack of affordable new quality housing certainly reflect the politics of selfish individualism and the politically short sightedness of a major shift to a service economy. The growth in privately appropriated urban spaces surrounded by office developments, particularly in London and major US cities, is now one suspects only temporarily suspended because of the bankrupt state of the incestuous closed cycle of institutional finance. The spectre of banks financing such centres for their own use, via the few international developers, while they squander massive funds elsewhere, causing their own developments to be jeopardised, is quite arrant.

> The song of canaries,
> never varies,
> And when they're moulting
> They're pretty revolting

(*Ogden Nash*, The Canary)

These self-centred centres through their urban infrastructure, architectural design and layered security systems, reject rather than enhance any natural integration with the surrounding urban and social fabric, and in some cases, such as Canary Wharf, physically injure the surrounding neighbourhood during construction and continue to do so long afterwards. Today there is a general recognition that autonomous endeavours based only on financial or political power in the built environment, particularly involving large scale projects, do not work well, and that they require wider collaboration and co-operation. More importantly, they need a shared and participatory commitment in order to create successful and sustainable development. Power can then be shared because the interests of all participants and those most affected are understood in a new context of a mutually acceptable development. This power shift moves towards those who are most affected in both the short and long term. Autonomy, in a democracy cannot exist. All levels of power, invested or imagined, exist within a framework of rights and responsibilities defined as much by others as by those who feel they have the power.

> The power is in the city council. The energy and initiative is in the local community. And if you put the initiative and power together, you can encourage the developer to make almost whatever you want.

(*Joan Busquets, former Director of Planning, Barcelona*)

Busquets refers to a moral power derived from the citizens.

There has been much talk of enablement (by 'enablers'). This is to enable the local communities to have more influence on their urban and social environment. What is more to the point is ennoblement of the citizen and the community. Ennoblement shifts the emphasis to respect, a recognition of the shift in power, rather than a rearguard action engineered by more socially responsible activists.

The architecture and urbanism of inner city developments can only be informed by the quality of the brief, derived from an understanding of local and city context and realised by the quality of the client. I would suggest its success is dependent on the client's moral power, whether the client is a developer, a local authority, a community group or partnership between any or all three, and the recognition that they are all 'clients' in some way.

Learning from Limehouse community

> Local communities should be more fully involved in the decisions which affect them. A 'top down' approach to regeneration does not seem to have worked. Local communities must be fully and effectively involved in planning, in the provision of local services, and in the managing and financing of specific projects. It is essential that people are encouraged to secure a stake in, feel a pride in, and have a sense of responsibility for their own area.

(*The Rt Hon Lord Scarman OBE*, The Brixton Disorders: Report on Inquiry into Causes of the 1981 Riots in Brixton)

> I do, however, welcome the concept of community based schemes and of development trusts to bring together all those concerned with and affected by redevelopment proposals. Major development, particularly in inner city areas, will not act as the catalyst for the community revitalisation which we are seeking unless it is acceptable both to the local planning authority and to those who live and work in the area.

(*Tom King, Minister for Local Government and Environmental Services, letter to LDG consultants URBED regarding Limehouse Basin proposals, 24 February 1982*)

> What we are trying to do is involve the people in the inner cities in a positive way.

(*Kenneth Baker, Secretary of State for the Environment*, BBC TV News, *1 December 1985*)

In 1980, I was involved, as a local resident, in establishing a local community development organisation after supporting a local campaign objecting to Commercial Road being transformed into a multi-laned ground level highway through Limehouse. This organisation, known as the Limehouse Development Group, identified in 1980 Limehouse Basin and the surrounding derelict land as the key to integrating Limehouse through a development strategy. This was in the light of the Thatcher government's political directive to state owned authorities to capitalise their under-used assets. The group's approach was to involve the local community (its residents and those who worked and owned businesses in the area), the local authority Tower Hamlets, the landowners and private developers in a coherent and collaborative approach to the regeneration of the area. In parallel we developed an engineered alternative underground traffic route through Limehouse in 1981, which was dismissed by the traffic planners at the GLC on the basis of the unachievable gradients for the road to rejoin the highway after passing under Limehouse Basin. The principle of an underground route was the only solution acceptable to local residents and businesses, and to Tower Hamlets.

Despite a financially viable community development proposal (Limehouse Basin) phased over several years, supported by development and construction industries and the local authority, the proposals were rejected by the British Waterways Board, owners of Limehouse Basin, who 'chose' an alternative private development scheme prepared by an ex-board member, which involved filling in nearly half of Limehouse Basin for luxury housing and offices, and which disregarded the surrounding neighbourhood. After a public enquiry held in Limehouse in 1983, the Government Inspector strongly urged that planning permission did not go ahead:

> The scheme would not integrate into the surrounding area but would reduce the overall integration of the area . . . I am convinced that the scheme would not properly advance the regeneration of this particular part of Docklands. I would recommend that it be refused.

(*Shane Rees LLB LMRTPI Solicitor Government Inspector for the Limehouse Basin Enquiry*, Report to the Secretary of State for the Environment, *June 1984*).

However, his recommendation was overruled fourteen months later in August 1985 by Patrick Jenkin, Secretary of State for the Environment during his last week in office.

This experience has not been forgotten by those who still live and work in Limehouse and its legacy has been a distrust of the democratic planning and public enquiry systems reinforcing a belief that even a public demonstration of democracy succumbs to hidden power.

. . . a design approach which completely ignores the existing setting, and which would in fact destroy it.
(*Peter Gibbs MA [Cantab] AA DipRIBA, Architectural Assessor for the Limehouse Basin*, Report to the Secretary of State for the Environment, *June 1984*)

In 1992, some private flats have been constructed in the south-west corner of the basin, many are unsold and unoccupied and no offices have been constructed. There is no clear development programme available from the developers or British Waterways Board. However, between 1989 and 1993 a new arterial road was constructed beneath Limehouse and the Basin, connecting the highway from the City with Canary Wharf and the east, avoiding major long term physical and environmental damage to Limehouse.

During the last decade we have, as local architects, attempted to help and learn from the local community in Limehouse through active involvement by:
– initiating urban discussions by suggesting a landscape strategy to help knit the physical environment together
– assessing community cultural needs (on behalf of the LDDC) while insisting that built facilities have the active participation of the local community and local authority
– designing a private development as an urban and landscape composition, with potential for future connection to the undeveloped surrounding area to the north, west and east
– providing knowledge and support to the local residents in their campaigns for a quieter and healthier environment to overcome the dramatic consequences of the new infrastructures constructed to serve the immense developments of London Docklands
– listening to and sometimes advising individuals and community groups.

We have learnt through our experiences with Limehouse and Poplar that neither a top down, nor bottom up approach is satisfactory in implementing inner city regeneration; an alternative which recognises a reality in which we are all citizens within a city (developer, financier, elected councillor, local resident, business person) and that successful environmental, social, economic development and regeneration is genuinely based on interdependence.

Previous page: View of Canary Wharf; *Above*: Aerial view of Limehouse
Basin, London (courtesy of Chorley & Handford Ltd)

NATURE AND PROPORTION

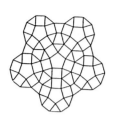
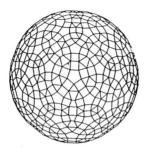

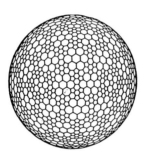

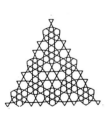
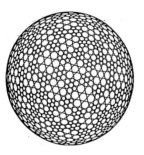

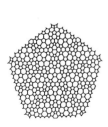
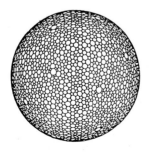

Chaos and complexity

It is interesting to conjecture that the western world's great artistic explosions since Greek times, ie the Renaissance and modern art, occurred following the discovery, or new perception of our Universe. Copernicus not only radically affected religion but prefaced the paradigm of art and humanism in the Renaissance; as did Einstein and others who created a new way for artists to perceive their work, which led to the great 20th-century mental construct of 'abstraction' which terminated our fixed view of geometry, and coincided with the beginning of the scientific age of 'certainty of uncertainty'. General relativity is a theory about geometry, or structure of space-time which has made us think not only in four dimensions but accept that space-time is also curved.

Architecture has been 'locked' geometrically into the Euclidean and Einsteinian constructs of space since the first decade of this century. Dr Walter Bauersfeld's geodesic design for Carl Zeiss at Jena, and Buckminster Fuller's later work demonstrated elegantly how geometrical relationships in curved space differ from those in flat space (two-dimensional). Does chaos, in particular its visual mathematical expression, fractals and fractal geometry, offer us a new way of looking at our sense of geometry and proportion in architecture? I think so. I would like to suggest that chaos is a renewal of interest in the mystery of nature, a rejection of Mondrian's right angle and his view of nature as random and capricious.

Despite Mondrian's approach, which has an inherent simplicity and certainly an ease of understanding in geometric and construction terms, a return to nature and its complexities is long overdue and fractal geometry at last gives our minds a new framework within which to theorise and experiment.

It is a truly contemporary way of describing our environment, but it does not yet offer us an explanation

which is complete and represents at one level a discovery which turns us back towards nature and at the same time is, along with preceding geometries, our current 'world' of geometry. It also provides a 'synthesis' in an economic age of analysis and compartmental isolation.

Fractal patterns, their symmetry across scale and fragmentation are visually seductive, but they are only new 'filters' on the world, in the same way that Euclidean and non-Euclidean geometries were and still are filters of information and 'motorways' for our minds. This is not to undermine the enormous release of creativity which fractal geometry gives to artists, scientists and others.

In a way, fractal mathematics is an attempt to describe nature's geometry, rather than previous mathematical geometries which described man's own geometric constructs. I would hazard a guess that what lies beyond fractal geometries can probably only be discovered when we better understand the multiverse (rather than universe).

The curved line, predominant in fractals recalls nature, the irregular; while the straight line is a more human construct and regular. The straight line appears distant from nature and the dominant art of the 20th century has paralleled man's 'dominant belief' over nature.

In essence, the 'irregular' phenomena of nature have always stimulated scientists, whether those exploring turbulent or fluctuating events such as the atmosphere or population. It was these types of events which the modern movement largely dismissed or ignored and whose reductivist and abstracted products the general public to a large extent rejected. Maybe there was a morphological aspect which was absent in this work which intuitively the general public sensed but could not define. Maybe the architecture of the modern movement always needed, as a palliative, a strong landscape to compensate for its lack of naturalness.

When Mandelbrot, Feigenbaum and others began exploring these irregular phenomena in nature, their work was a more holistic appreciation of natural phenomena and eventually led to a science of the nature of systems (chaos), addressing complex behaviour and in particular, everyday events rather than highly specialised areas of research such as particle physics.

Largely through the beautiful patterns of fractal geometry, general interest in chaos theory and complexity has increased. Attempts to connect a theory of beauty, or even art, to a theory of complex natural phenomena, chaos, seems to be suggested in some way through the observation of subtle changes, small variations, and these can be seen in self-similar pattern scale shifts of fractal geometry.

Studies of spiral phenomena in nature before the 20th century, whether on the surface of certain shells, hidden within the cell structure of plants or the growth of leaves on a stem sometimes reveal a scale shift of spiral similarity.

Spirals in the 19th century were approximated mathematically to the logarithmic spiral construction as an abstract conception of perfect growth as seen in nature (cf also Fibonacci series 1, 2, 3, 5, 8 13; and study of the clouds from Leonardo's sketches for *The Deluge*).

Initial design experiments in architecture as responses to chaos theory and fractals, have seen the re-emergence of the curve, both in plan and section. Is this a renewed concern with the geometric poetry seen in nature? The other has been deconstruction, which essentially displaces man (and his conventional constructs) from the centre or focus. This counters Mondrian's 'right angle dominance of nature' and is more concerned with complexity as a visual experience. Deconstruction does not attempt, yet, to engage natural processes and living materials, but remains tethered to the construction materials of the modern movement, in particular constructivist materials.

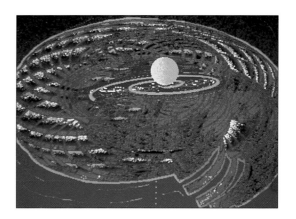

Previous page left: Explored geometries for Pearl of the Gulf, Dubai (Ensor Holiday, Keith Laws); France-Japan Ring: annular vessel of carbon coated woven titanium levitated by supermagnets and restrained by small diameter titanium rods. Its 'active skin' responds in colour to the original global network game – the 'poiesis generator' (copyright Olivier Auber); *Previous page right*: Pearl of the Gulf; *Above*: Poiesis Generator; *Right*: Ecology Gallery, Natural History Museum, London

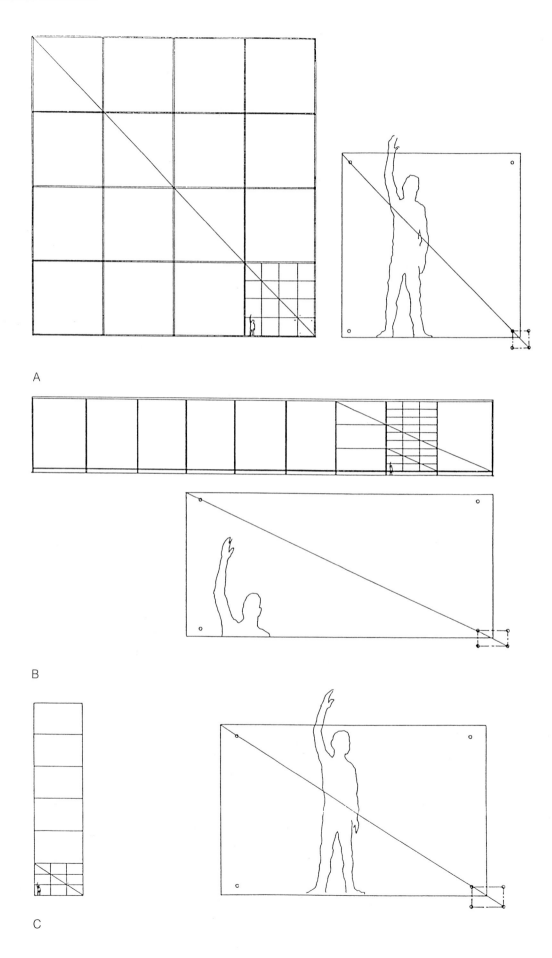

A

B

C

Geometry, hierarchy and scale

At the heart of three-dimensional creativity lies geometry. The re-emergence of nature as a source reawakens an appreciation of the Greek proportions and geometric techniques, not of Euclidean geometry but in our present interest in the curved line. Vertical and horizontal entasis suggested an understanding of the way the human brain translated straight lines. This divergence from mathematical regularity, which is also characteristic of Gothic Cathedral architecture, is possibly related not only to perception but perhaps related also to wider appreciations of nature.

Geodesic spheres create a more intuitive delight as the frequency of the subdivision increases, ie as they approximate closer and closer to spherical curvature, and nature (compound eye, etc). In our own projects, working with Ensor Holiday and Keith Laws (1983-85) on new spherical geometries other than those based on triangulation, this phenomenon was very evident. In fact, our desire to use two-dimensional geometries which were not so familiar on spherical surfaces was also an intuitive response to enable the perceived curvature to be more fluid, whilst at the same time achieving a complexity of surface pattern (visual mathematics) eg Pearl of Dubai, where we also sought a strong reference to arabesque geometries.

The importance of scale shift, the perception of the overall form and increasing the viewer's awareness that a geometric hierarchy is the basic compositional element of our work began to appear clearly through our work with Peter Rice and Martin Francis on the La Villette facades and has been continued through the B8 Building at Stockley Park, Reina Sofia Museum of Modern Art and Magdalen College.

The other crucial aspect in these compositions is that the degree of visual complexity of the constructional elements also increases as the viewer approaches closer to the building, whilst maintaining the basic geometry. This visual complexity is achieved in different ways. It can be in the complexity of form of the components as they decrease, or by introducing other geometric shapes and forms, eg circles within squares, cylinders within cubes, the twisting of planes, introduction of compound organic curves. These hierarchical constructs are not fractal, ie self-similar objects and effective dimension, but quite a close allegory: the repetition of proportional relationships at shifted scales whose random periods are visually determined by the desired dimensions of the major common denominator tempered by its technical limits, often the glass cladding panel.

The importance of a determined hierarchy is that it gives the viewer a framework within which his scale and that of the building can meet and be tangible at different distances, and that the experience offers sustained interest, didactic or intellectual/aesthetic content as the viewer moves around close to the building. This is generally much more evident in historical architecture.

It is important that our architecture does reflect the human scale and responds to human perception, whether a person is static or moving at a hundred kilometres per hour, and whether the person is one kilometre or one metre away.

Previous page left: Graphic hierarchy – large/small scale, from distance/close-up: **A** bioclimatic facades, La Villette, Paris; **B** Building B8, Stockley Park, London; **C** Reina Sofia Museum of Modern Art, Madrid; *Previous page right*: Glass satellite tower detail, Reina Sofia Museum of Modern Art; *Opposite*: B8 Building, Stockley Park, Heathrow

ART

Preconcepts

The prerequisite to establishing our approach to a new project is a preconcept. This is not to be mistaken for a concept informing the design and guiding the detail development of the architecture. For us, a preconcept engages the most informed holistic view which we can describe, and uses expressions such as poetry to capture the essence of the project under consideration. This initial stage is the most crucial in establishing the foundation of the project.

For example, Eagle Rock house, which we designed for Ursula Colahan in 1981, was, in the client's mind, discussed some years earlier during a conversation in Italy. The discussion centred around her hypothetical return to England and her desire to travel the world in search of exotic plants, particularly orchids. This led to a metaphor of a parent bird and the potential for that bird, whose young had flown the nest, to redefine home as 'being on the wing carrying a suitcase'. To me, there was no portrayal of permanence, only of 'freedom of move-ment with minimum physical encumbrance'. This conver-sation took place in a wonderful atmosphere of fiction as far as I was concerned at the time, but revealed much about her dreams. My perception of her hypothetical objectives was not to do with the architecture of a house, or even a home, but that her life could in some way be liberated from material concerns and responsibilities. Years later, when she did decide to sell many of her possessions and house in Italy, her actions seemed to be consistent with those perceived points of our discussion. Only her desire to be sometimes physically nearer some of her friends, who were in England, confirmed that the initial conversation had tentative roots in reality. How-ever, her idea of an English base carried no architectural prejudice. In fact the nearest notion she had to a physical base was a 'barn'. When we first saw the site together

Far right: Initial concept for France-Japan Ring (computer simulation graphics, Guilhem Pratz)

upon which Eagle Rock was ultimately built, I suggested that the small yellow cottage, which occupied the only ground space above which the sky was entirely visible, be removed, to allow the site's beautiful natural qualities to be better appreciated. It was at this moment, inspired both by the site and the cottage, that a first shift in perception occurred. She stated that the cottage should go because it wasn't big enough – big enough for what exactly, I queried. The suggestion implicit in her remark was clearly a desire for tangible living accommodation, almost immediately confirmed by her in terms of square footage. So the latent preconcept of 'flight and freedom of movement', perceived by me as the essential nature of this individual client, met the nature of the physical site and the certainty of a base.

The design concept for this base began as a series of isolated timber containers set down, as one would a base camp: one for sleeping, one for cooking, one for storage and another for hygiene, all beneath a transparent ('sky') protective canopy from wind, rain and snow. I felt that she might, and that the site could, accept these discreet objects.

Ultimately, the need was for a house and home – to be lived in more or less permanently. The preconcept pervaded the design concept and in the end highlighted the fiction of the original dream of flight and freedom. The design developed into an anchored sculpture, as a metaphor of a wing-clipped bird, underlying to me the importance of the preconcept as a personal reference for the architecture, and not a fixed agreement or idea.

The Ecology Gallery's preconcept was 'man in a fragile environment', inspired by the very first impressions of the nature of Waterhouse's masterpiece, the Natural History Museum, and our desire not to physically touch it, and by the meaning of 'ecology'.

Preconcepts are defined from the essence of the initial situation, and in our approach to architecture this is distilled from as whole a picture as we can 'perceive' at the time. It is concerned with our perception of the needs, desires and aspirations of our client, and is subjective and creative. Often this initial situation is without a known site or a known user.

Essence

Since most of our education and learning has come through words, written and spoken, there is a need to unravel much which is camouflaging our ability to access the essence of situations. The amount of information which enters our brains is roughly split 90/10, eyes /ears. Poetry and a living poet can often provide the opportunity to catch another bus to another destination – ie, a different view and a different way of using language.

When one looks at a painting by Turner, for example, the power and dynamic of light is such that the object content is almost incidental. Similarly, looking at a photograph of a construction by Goldsworthy, the essence of nature's site, form, material and transience is captured beautifully by his skill and respect for the environment he is in.

Brancusi's 'bird in space' or 'head' captures only the essential, the cycle of life from egg to form.

Working with artists and poets, and others like the engineer Peter Rice, one can be guided through the issues and context to the essentials, and not the relationships of the project, which have by their very nature a complexity which can confuse.

Adieu, dit le renard. Voici mon secret. Il est tres simple: on ne voit bien qu'avec le coeur. L'essentiel est invisible pour les yeux.

[Goodbye, said the fox. Here is my secret. It is very simple: one can only see well with the heart. The essential is invisible to the eyes.]

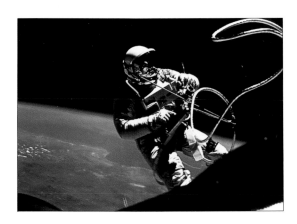
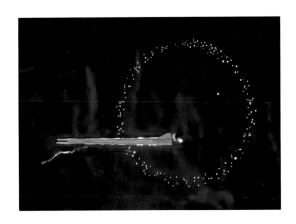

Above: La Villette facade, looking up; *Opposite*: Reina Sofia Museum of
Modern Art, Madrid; *Overleaf left*: National Maritime Museum of the Boat,
London, concept drawing; *Overleaf right*: Concept vignettes for Eagle Rock

(*Antoine de St-Exupery*, Le Petit Prince, *1940*)

In contrast, Le Corbusier's expressed view was: 'Art is in its essence arrogant.' (*Le Corbusier*, Towards a New Architecture, *1923*)

Concepts

Our architectural concepts should emerge from the preconcept, informing and providing the framework for developing the architectural design.

The development of any one of our projects can be contained by a singular concept but also by a set of ideas which are coalesced and understood as a hierarchy of concepts, all reinforcing each other. The hierarchy of concepts for the Reina Sofia glass circulation towers, for example, were:
– solidity and transparency
– gravitas and lightness
– history and modernity
– minimalism and complexity
and to reveal, didactically, the structural composition and behaviour.

The importance of describing a concept(s) at the beginning of the design process is to provide the reference point for various explorations of form, volume, light, energy, structure, surface, and organisation through which we can 'measure' the potential latent energy in the concept(s).

It is essential for us to gauge this potential energy store early in order that we can confirm or refute the strength of the concept(s), and its ability to sustain our involvement and that of our client and collaborators throughout the duration of the project.

There is no denying that there exists, in all projects, a more or less difficult assault course to negotiate, and that it is important for us to recognise the 'energy level' required to be successful, and that the journey can be enjoyed by all involved.

Our ability to imagine and construct concepts is at the very root of our architecture, and without them there can be no architecture, only building. The majority of them rely on abstract notions derived from nature, and occasionally concrete ideas, in the sense of having no reference to nature, history or architecture but to mental constructs.

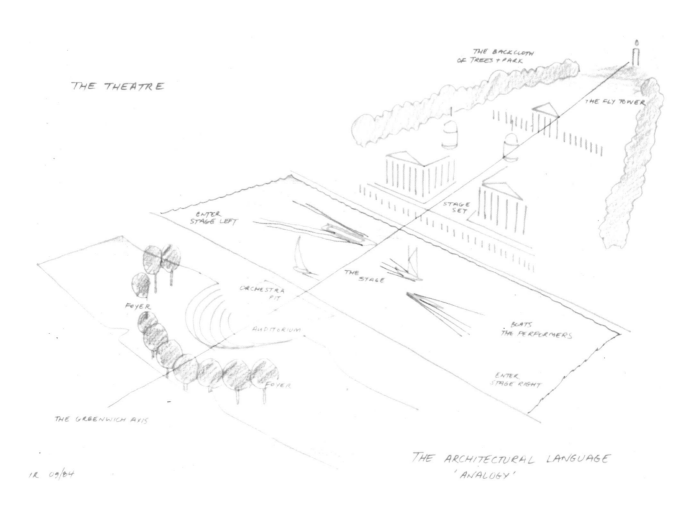

THE THEATRE

THE ARCHITECTURAL LANGUAGE
'ANALOGY'

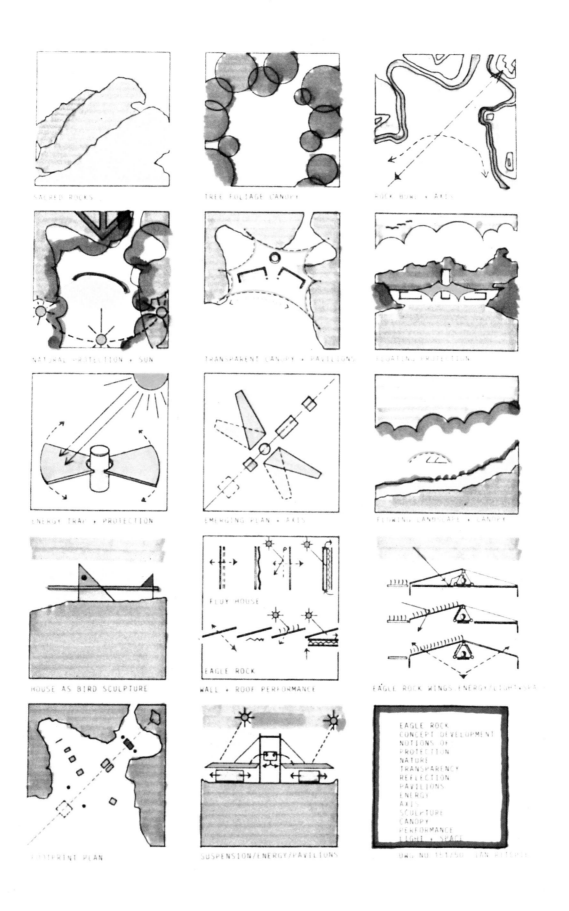

SACRED ROCKS

TREE FOLIAGE CANOPY

ROCK BOWL + AXIS

NATURAL PROTECTION + SUN

TRANSPARENT CANOPY + PAVILIONS

FLOATING PROTECTION

ENERGY TRAP + PROTECTION

EMERGING PLAN + AXIS

FLOWING LANDSCAPE + CANOPY

HOUSE AS BIRD SCULPTURE

WALL + ROOF PERFORMANCE

EAGLE ROCK WINGS ENERGY/LIGHT+SEA

FOOTPRINT PLAN

SUSPENSION/ENERGY/PAVILIONS

EAGLE ROCK
CONCEPT DEVELOPMENT
NOTIONS OF
PROTECTION
NATURE
TRANSPARENCY
REFLECTION
PAVILIONS
ENERGY
AXIS
SCULPTURE
CANOPY
PERFORMANCE
LIGHT + SPACE

DWG NO 151250 IAN RITCHIE

SCIENCE AND TECHNOLOGY

Scientific understanding

Our world is still dominated by the scientific culture and applied technology despite an increasing questioning of the validity of this cultural reality. This questioning is strongly related to the ever-increasing change in the rate of change brought about by man's ingenuity and exploitation of scientific understanding and technology.

The depth of knowledge in so many areas of study is such that there can no longer again be an individual universal man in the Renaissance sense, but this is no excuse for not wanting to understand. In architecture and engineering, the science of matter and materials, forces, energy and power, of processed materials, transportation and communications, the atmosphere and the earth, and the quality and techniques of measurement and analysis are all important. Yet these are scientific models, constructed by man to better describe the world. How we use these models and their inter-connectedness, is informed by our cultural education and by our environment.

> We are in the midst of a transformation of the building industry. Arts and crafts are being replaced by science and technology – or should I say science-guided design and mechanised production. Science-guided design and mechanised production technology for short – is the domain of engineers.

(*Ove Arup Institute of Civil Engineering, 26 October 1972*)

This may be largely true, but somehow the dominance of this domain by engineers and the incapacity of architects and artists to influence design, either through ignorance of the materials and processes or lack of collaborative opportunity, has collectively made us, in part, responsible for the lack of quality in much of our built environment. But Arup's statement is also a reflection of the post-war society concerned with efficient industrial production to rebuild the housing and industrial

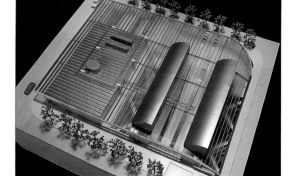

Above: Drawing for Bermondsey Station, Jubilee Line Extension (hierarchy: structure/fitting, rough/smooth); *Right*: Bermondsey Station model, glass fixing and interior perspective

fabric of our cities. This industrial efficiency subsequently became part of the commercial imperative which has dramatically contributed to the depressing character of so many city centres.

If engineers and architects consider themselves designers (although not many are), then both must be aware of the *aims* (what and for whom) and the *means* (how) to reach quality solutions. Too often the engineer is only concerned with the *means*, remaining unconcerned and ignorant of the wider *aims*, while the architect faced with unfamiliar techniques and materials loses confidence and security in his position as 'leader' of the design team and essentially abdicates, with the consequence that the wider *aims* never materialise.

A classic illustration of this schism still being reinforced was the contract brief we received from London Underground Ltd, Jubilee Line Extension for the design of Bermondsey Station. For the engineers the project objectives were to construct the project as rapidly as possible, and to construct and operate with minimum disturbance to local infrastructure, communities and the environment. For us, as architects, there were two additional project objectives: to provide a modern railway for the 21st century, meeting the best possible standard of safety, performance and quality and to provide an agreeable environment that recognises increasing customer expectations.

Divorcing the civil engineers from these two fundamental project objectives demonstrates the practice of design apartheid habitual in architecture and engineering and creates a totally unnecessary obstacle course to achieving a collaborative, enjoyable and quality solution.

To what extent do we as architects have an ethical obligation to understand such scientific diversity? Architecture is perhaps one of the few 'professions' which should bridge the scientific and artistic cultures.

There is no doubt that our ecological awakening demands that our decisions are based on a better understanding of scientific and technical knowledge. Even today we should not have to be specialists to understand scientific language (though a reasonable grasp of numeracy is very useful). It should also be incumbent on scientists to write comprehensibly. How as architects do we organise this knowledge and access it intelligently?

We have to establish cross-scientific links with the research and development world, industry and our fellow collaborators in project design and realisation. Fortunately, the growth in available information and knowledge is paralleled with that in data storage, retrieval and speed of communication. This, in tandem with a more information-free environment, should enable us to access and evaluate scientific and technical knowledge pertinent to the ingredients and application of our architecture. 'Us', in this context, does not mean architects alone, or even with other professionals working together. The expertise input and analysis is and needs to be even broader; scientists, production engineers, artists and the users should take part in an informed choice.

In order to be effective as architects we have to be genuinely interested and informed, and in the process we seek enjoyment. This 'joy' comes from the enlightenment we receive through the process, the appropriate knowledge we obtain, and the success we see in integrating this new personal and shared understanding to the architectural design and its realisation. Our enjoyment often rubs off on all those involved and usually makes for a better result. If as architects we have no genuine interest, then science and technology will be represented only as an uninformed image, predetermined by industrial prejudice and politic, and will in no sense be tamed by our ethical and aesthetic obligation and responsibility to serve society better. Somehow,

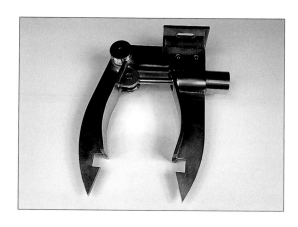

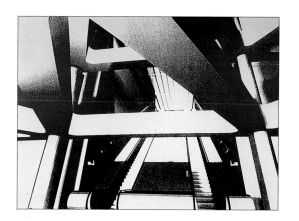

science through education must be demystified for architects as much as for the general population. Science is not just about 'certainty', it is also about conjectures and doubts. Today, science is increasingly having to face the moral and ethical quicksand of our time.

Scientific understanding of the principles of how things behave and work is crucial to our architectural designs, enabling us to evaluate and use appropriate materials, products and systems in each unique physical and social environmental context of our projects. This knowledge through the depth of analysis reduces the risk of errors, compared to the all too easy acceptance of specifications and performance from existing products. It may appear on the surface that in some projects we are behaving like Icarus, but we do prepare our parachutes!

> *Or, peu de siècles présentent autant que le nôtre une série de progrès scientifiques d'une valeur incontestable . . . Nos architectes, comme leurs devanciers, vont-ils s'empresser de recourir à cette source de rénovation? Non; ils préfèrent nier l'influence nécessaire de la science sur l'art et nous donner des monuments de style bàtard, plus ou moins inspiré de l'architecture de décadence des deux derniers persistent à nier ainsi la lumière, à refuser à la science le concours qu'elle ne demande qu'à leur prêter, les architectes ont fini leur rôle; celui des ingénieurs commence, c'est-à-dire le rôle des hommes adonnés au constructions, qui partiront des connaissances purement scientifiques pour composer un art déduit de ces connaissances et des nécessités imposées par notre temps.*

(*Viollet-Le-Duc, Entretiens sur l'Architecture, 1863*)

Structural engineering is the science and art of designing and making, with economy and elegance, buildings, bridges, frameworks, and other

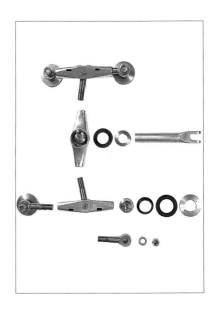

Above: The glass roof, vertical 'walls' and floor of suspended Lintas Bridge, Paris, 1984 (photograph, Alain Guisdard); *Below*: 'H' fixing for La Villette Museum of Science, Paris; *Opposite*: View of La Villette with bioclimatic facades; Cultural and Sports Centre, Albert, France

similar structures so that they can safely resist the forces to which they may be subjected.
(*Institute of Structural Engineering, UK – definition*)

The engineer, inspired by the law of economy and governed by mathematical calculation, puts us in accord with universal law. He achieves harmony.
(*Le Corbusier*, Towards a New Architecture, *1923*)

Le Corbusier's optimism must have been based on the seduction of lightweight engineering inventiveness in aeronautical and automotive engineering in the first two decades of this century, for how rare in our building industry is the structural or civil engineer who fits this description.

Numbers

'Numbers,' (to quote John McLeish) 'are not a sadistic conspiracy devised by one half of society for torturing the other half.' If we add culture to this number source, then we really do create the medium of invention.

In everyday existence numbers can be seen as concrete in the sense that they are used as symbols describing the quantity of objects. In mathematical geometry, numbers result from an abstract method of describing spatial relationships, whose interest to me is the relationship between the numbers rather than the numbers themselves.

In Euclidean geometry these relationships are defined within prescribed forms, which have defined boundaries and space, and which can be 'seen and touched'.

In modern mathematics, points in space, for example, can be described by sets of numbers corresponding to x, y and z coordinates and space itself having n-dimensions. This is but one universal method of describing spatial relationships. These mathematical descriptions are abstract (non-object based), and become complex and much less tangible, and yet like geometric forms are

inventions of the mind. Certain art in the early 20th century was also non-object based (Suprematism – Malevich's black square which could be read as zero, and the white square as infinity). This art is not to be confused with Cubism which essentially abstracted natural objects in order to be able to look at the object afresh.

Modern mathematics was an immense conceptual shift, which by unlocking our object-based perception of the world has allowed a flowering in both mathematics and the arts. Non-Euclidean geometry and the fourth dimension is a mind game (whether understood as time: liberation from conventional linear perspective; abstract space mathematically described as four mutually perpendicular axes; or philosophically as a physical hyperspace which we cannot 'touch or see') – a game not based on our visual senses, which is why it appears alien to everyday existence. Mathematics uses imagination and logic in much the same way as our architectural creativity relies on the interaction of intuition and intellect. An interesting comparison was experienced while designing elements of Reina Sofia – the union of hand and eye in describing and judging intuitively the 'rightness' of a curved line, and the balance between this and the reliance on numerical 'analogues' by computer. The introduction of time, dynamics and energy in modern mathematics has changed our perception of static objects, giving them time-relative spatial constructs, and has embraced change as an integral part of mathematically described reality.

Art, too, became for some synonymous with mathematical concepts of space-time (eg, kinetic art of Moholy-Nagy/Calder, Pierre Henri's 'music concrete', Kubric's 2001) as pure constructions of the mind and not about describing observable phenomena.

This commentary introduces the context of the present-day application of modern mathematics to

From above: Cable bracing of the glass facades, La Villette (photograph, Alain Guisdard); Instruments measuring tension of the fabric roof, La Villette; 'Dolphin' suspension arm, Reina Sofia Museum of Modern Art, Madrid; Wind resistance fitting, Reina Sofia

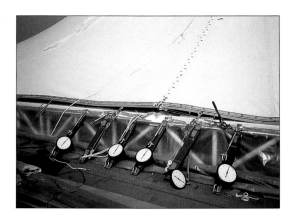

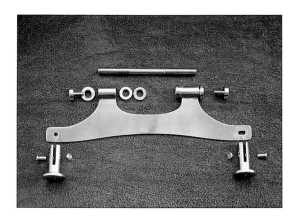

natural phenomena which we can perceive and which we are now attempting to describe with numbers. Man's desire to describe these phenomena is initially one of curiosity, but will no doubt lead to new ways of imagining and of simulating them in various fields of application. Some of the research in simulating hydrodynamic flow (eg Alistair Day's work at Ove Arup + Partners) led to a new level of understanding in the application of tensioned fabric structures. The use of non-linear structural analysis afforded a new appreciation of structural behaviour and at La Villette this enabled RFR, supported by Ove Arup + Partners, to develop the structural 'flexibility' and finesse of the structure by accepting greater deflections than normal in the cable bracing of the glass facades. Non-linear analysis recognises that the final geometry under load is different from the initial geometry by such an amount that its behaviour is different, and that 'restoration' is a characteristic of stability.

A great deal of painting (Piero della Francesca) and architecture was based on the laws of Euclidean geometry – considering regular bodies as theoretically perfect forms and whose compositional relationships were thought to reveal and reproduce the underlying order of nature. History provides plenty of evidence of integrated mathematical and artistic works and collaboration. During the Renaissance, the artist was very often the best practising mathematician as well as the most accomplished theoretician. Today, mathematicians are using visualisations facilitated by computer graphic techniques to look anew at phenomena, (eg, new minimal surfaces); equally, artists are researching new forms and relationships through these new technologies. These instruments allow collaborative experiments in mathematics and art ('Renaissance revisited') in a dimension and time frame that are quite new.

'Visual mathematics' offers a real opportunity to

reintegrate art and science in specific areas, particularly geometries, three-dimensional surfaces and quite obviously architecture.

In our architecture we are interested with the idea of 'spaces becoming' (dynamic-changing), rather than just 'spaces being' (static); based on an understanding that everyone can perceive space differently at different times. This notion can be described and analysed through space-time visualisation using computer animation, although the simultaneous presentation of several 'flight paths' in continuously varying light and levels of visibility in new spatial constructs and surfaces is still to become available. We have recently for the Leipzig Glass Hall explored certain dynamic spatial characteristics (ventilation, smoke) and human behaviour (escape) using VR/ fluid dynamic software with Keith Stills (Colt International).

> Mathematics, rightly viewed, possesses not only truth, but supreme beauty – a beauty cold and austere, like that of sculpture.

(*Bertrand Russell*, Mysticism and Logic, *1918*)

Materials

When Robert Filliou walked through the streets of Paris in the early 60s with his 'museum in a hat', artists such as Oldenberg placed objects out of context in situations where their scale relationship was surreal, and Warhol celebrated the consumer product. The general public and the conservative art world were predictably outraged. These controversial statements were made in order to challenge western society's complacency.

Today, in the construction industry, after decades dominated by the power of industrial production of monotonous products resulting from management and manufacturing methods seeking ever more economies, there is now a need to inject art into industry. The design, engineering and manufacture of primary materials into

products which carry the signature of the designer, the presence of the human hand, mind and heart has become essential in order that industry not only serves man's material needs, but also his sensibilities.

Some of our work has and will continue to be controversial in the sense of making industry rethink its attitude, challenging its dominance while at the same time attempting to achieve those human qualities in material products through their scale, position and contribution to the overall architecture. In order to communicate this to the industries with whom we work, it is necessary to acquire a deep understanding of the true nature of materials, to learn how to manipulate these materials in an aesthetic manner and to appreciate how industry can produce the products from them.

This approach is not that of taking industrial products from other industries (marine, aerospace) and executing an aesthetic technological transfer, or taking society's industrial waste to produce one-off architectural art pieces, but is an approach which seeks to infect industry in its own home with these human and sensible values. We believe it is here that change is necessary which will allow new architectures to emerge. This approach recognises the role of industry in our society, utilises the creative and economic potential of computers and computer-controlled machines to provide the necessary products to serve society's needs through tailor-made volume production, and not just for the private and privileged indulgence of a few. This potential to link computer aided design to numerically controlled machine production to fabricate one-offs by the thousand, quickly and efficiently, redefines the old economic argument of industrial mass production of the construction industry and allows art direct access to production.

An architecture which uses materials to reflect the condition of society, where these materials are used in

Below left to right: Conceptual interior, Meridian Planetarium, Greenwich; Poiesis Generator; Ecology Gallery bridge, Natural History Museum, London; Culling Road shaft, Jubilee Line Extension

their primary state rather than as products, eg metal sheet coil, and engages craftsmen to manipulate them, with or without the use of computers, in the factory or in their site assembly, can represent a late 20th-century evolution of the Arts and Crafts tradition. This approach has its place in today's age in the sense of humanising processed materials, at a small scale, but in my opinion does not address the larger issue where the construction industry and its products have more pervasive effect in the built environment. This predominantly urban environment is largely created by architects acting as 'aesthetic' purchasing agents, sometimes good, but more often poor, simply acquiring on behalf of their clients the construction of the vast majority of corporate, institutional and commercial buildings. The kitsch and neo-traditional use of materials and products to create a veneer architecture violate our senses in a way that truly historic buildings never do.

It is crucial to remember that architecture is a very important forum for the ever evolving development of our technical culture, and we have been very fortunate to have worked with, and to be inspired by engineers, in particular, Peter Rice.

I am interested in the ways in which the engineer can help to bring back some of the joy and excitement which characterises many of the buildings we admire from the past . . . This brings to mind another myth about technology. The feeling that technological choice is always the result of a predetermined logic. The feeling that there is a correct solution to a technical question is very common. But a technical solution like any other decision is a moment in time. It is not definitive. It is a moment in time and place where the people, their background and their talent is paramount. What is often missing is the evidence of human intervention,

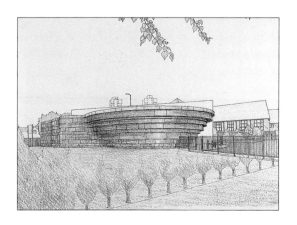

the black box syndrome. So by looking at new materials, or at old materials in a new way we change the rules. People become visible again. (*Peter Rice*, An Engineer's View, *RIBA, June 1992*)

'Life without industry is guilt, and industry without art is brutality' (*John Ruskin, lecture on Art 3*: The Relation of Art to Morals, *23 February 1870*)

Light

'Our earth is simply the natural greenhouse of our solar system home, sustained by sunlight and the magic of photosynthesis . . . An en-lightened environment is what we all seek, politically, eco-nomically and physically.' (*IR Ingolstadt, Light + Architecture exhibition catalogue, September 1992*)

Without light there is no architecture. The history of architecture has been the story of light as the essential material of architecture. Today we can look back and see how architectural interiors have been created: first by allowing light to penetrate through openings in solid walls, then through small openings in the roof, and at the beginning of the 20th century walls were removed, and today, almost at will we can remove the roof. The exceptional work of Paxton (and others) remains an enigma, having removed the solidity of the entire building envelope in the mid-19th century.

Our dominion over the physical envelope of our buildings using glass is not matched by our ability to control and compose with light, whether it is diffused, direct or indirect sunlight or artificial, yet the means to do so are now as never before available to us. It is important to understand that the absence of light makes light alive – nature's cycles day to night and the changing qualities of natural light through the seasons are constant reminders.

By understanding solar geometry we can recapture the art of carving form and the surfaces of buildings with nature's own light pen. To understand light enables us to spatially create a dynamic to tranquil range of atmospheres.

Transparent envelopes accept natural light as it is, with its continuously changing qualities, modifying it spectrally as it passes through glass. Transparency is rarely an architectural composition of light but a dynamic saturation of space, a situation which nearly always requires the control of the quantity (and sometimes the quality) of sunlight by shading. Shading design can consequently create a strong external or internal architectural composition. Transparency is simultaneously the negation of light and its totality.

In our architecture, understanding the symbiotic relationship of glass and light is crucial. Having explored glass technically over the past few years our attention is now equally focused on light, its energy and colour content.

Natural phenomena such as firefly-lucifer, cold bioluminescent light-emitter, nature's own photonic communicator; mirage; virtual reality are some of the areas of research which interest us. So too have been reflector systems and holograms to control, focus and distribute light directly into spaces, or through light pipes. As we pipe water, fossil energy, air, information and waste through our buildings, it seems inevitable that there are advantages in piping light efficiently. Consequently, this should enable us to be more intelligent with the energy performance of our architectural envelopes and spaces.

In 1947 Dennis Gabor at Imperial College, London, postulated that three-dimensional images (holograms) could be created from electron beams or x-rays. Today laser technology, the control of light in '2D', primarily operating in the visible light spectrum, provides society with an exceptional range of tools.

With J-L Lhermitte, Francois Bastien and the EDF at Clamart, Paris, we experimented with the idea of the

Opposite: Stonehenge, Wiltshire; Metal screened hologram (Institute of Light, Cologne)

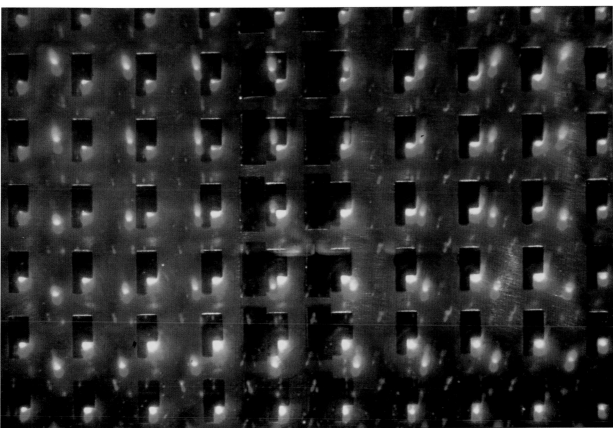

three-dimensional control of light. In a near vacuum (0.04 to ten millibars), electrical energy was discharged from different shaped cathodes in an eight-metre-high cylindrical glass tube. Rings and bird forms were created. To forecast any application useful to society of this would be to speculate about the nature of man's future journeys in space!

Light is apparently both wave and particle, and until recently demonstrated at the laboratories of Hamamatsu Photonics, analysis of photons had never revealed these behavioural characteristics simultaneously. Now the accepted 'wholeness' of Quantum Theory has been undermined. There is a long way to go to understand light as a material and this research 'mirrors' the research at sub-atomic levels to better understand the nature and versatility of glass.

The wonder of glass – transparency

In architecture, glass has for a thousand years been the medium through which light has entered buildings revealing the spatial art of architecture, while completing the building's protective enclosure of walls and roof against the elements while allowing visual contact to be maintained with the outside world.

Glass is a beautiful chaotic solid, whose ubiquity is a witness to its material versatility and man's ingenuity, limited only by our incomplete understanding of its material nature. It is a material based on silica, seeded with metal oxides which can render it transparent and opaque, black and white or virtually any degree between either of these limits. If one looks perpendicularly at a transparent form of it, it is not there, yet its impermeability can control the passage of air, water, noise, dirt and energy: a window between us and our environment, whether we are stationary or at high speed, in a comfortable or very extreme environment. It has particular

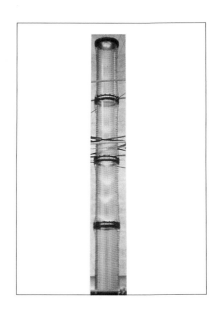

From above: Light-transmitting, glass fibre fabric roof of La Villette Museum under construction; Light installation for 'Light and Architecture' exhibition, Ingolstadt; Vacuum glass tube used to experiment with three-dimensional control of light (photograph, J-L Lhermitte)

physical strengths and by processing it can possess great structural performance and resistance. Glass is reasonably energy efficient in capital terms because it is spread thinly, is recyclable and sourced from an abundant supply making it relatively acceptable ecologically.

When its atomic structure and its momentary ordered geometry is fully understood, and if its vulnerability to crack propagation can be mastered, then this 5000 year old material will enter a new phase of magnificent service to man in the fields of architecture, art, telecommunications and industrial products.

The history of making glass has seen five main stages, two by the hand and so far three by machine: the working of molten glass as it cools and becomes more viscous and the blowing of molten glass to produce thin walled vessels and the first 'flat' glass; the machine production of vessels (bottles, mid-19th century), the production of large flat sheets by the 'float' process in the 50s (revolutionising our built environment), and more recently the production of glass fibres (revolutionising the quantity and speed of our communication). The latter in woven form has also helped to create a new architectural material.

Our innovatory work with Peter Rice and Martin Francis (RFR) at La Villette dealt primarily with two different material forms of glass: flat and transparent, and glass fibre fabric.

We believed that the bioclimatic facades as windows to the park were also windows into the museum, and as such transparency was a concept worth developing. It is this concept, and the defining of transparency which became the major objective. Transparency suggests the invisible, yet it was clear to us that the structure of the facades would be anything but invisible seen from within the museum. It was the clear glass plane which would represent the transparent window, and this suggested a visual relationship to the structure where the structure would 'appear' to support nothing apart from itself. Of course if this was possible, then the logic of having a structure at all would be questioned. The way we defined the existence of the transparent surface when viewed from inside and outside would be crucial to the successful realisation of our concept of transparency. We concluded that the external surface of the glass surface should be flush, which informed us that the mechanical fixing of the glass should lie within the plane of the glass itself, or inside it, thus visibly identifying the transparent surface. Equally, how people actually look, (the eye scans more easily horizontally) suggested that the facades should have a horizontal emphasis creating clear panoramas. This indicated to us the way we should design the structural wind load systems.

The very particular technical innovation which contributed so much to the successful realisation of the concept of transparency was in the smallest of all the components, the glass suspension assembly which transfers, under normal conditions, the accumulated load of four glass panels to the primary structure. The failure scenario of two adjacent top glass panels breaking simultaneously, together with the refusal of the checking authority to accept that the shear load capacity of the vertical silicone joints would contribute to stability, meant that the single top suspension glass hole required proof of its capacity to carry in excess of 4000 kilogrammes. In 1983, this was seven times greater than the proven experience of international glass industries. This problem was solved, through the machining tolerance of the glass hole and the introduction of a spherical bearing lying within the thickness of the glass, which eliminated localised stresses from glass bending under wind load. The final design of this component, as intended, was flush with the external glass surface and small in scale. The 80s phenomena of built 'transparent glass architecture' originates from our project, although most of them have relied on the principle of a simple countersunk screw fixing through glass carrying much less load, limited by the intense concentration of local stress around the screw head due to bending in the glass or its support.

In the detailed design engineering of the facades we considered other important ideas, eg tension (symbolising 'technology with or versus nature'), their didactic role, geometric hierarchy, scale shift to create complexity and visual richness as component assemblies became smaller, approaching the scale of the human hand.

Above the entrance hall we created a 2,000-square-metre roof of glass fibre fabric, in which were placed two rotating truncated cylindrical domes containing parallel arrays of computer controlled mylar mirrors tracking and rotating to reflect the sun's rays into the entrance hall. Our concept was to provide legible hierarchies of structure and light. We felt that the lighting should decrease in intensity from the central areas of the domes towards the perimeter of the entrance hall, in much the same way as the structure. To achieve this we designed a translucent, but thermally insulated fabric roof (K: 0.6W/m^2/°C). This was composed of two skins of different densities of Teflon coated glass fibre, insulated with 300 millimetres of white spun glass fibres (Fibair) supported on a transparent vapour barrier of Tedlar film. Between the insulation and outer structural skin was a ventilated air space. The structural fabric's primary advantage is that it is permanent, and secondly, it allows a certain transmission of light. Overall, the structural fabric composite roof transmitted approximately three per cent of incident light. This was the first application of a thermally insulated and ventilated light-transmitting glass fibre fabric roof.

In contrast to our structural use of glass at La Villette was our research into three-dimensional forming and treatment of glass to create a symbol, the Pearl, to help communicate Dubai's emergence as the cultural centre of the Gulf. We sought to establish an 'arabesque' geometry for both the structure and the glazing, and several were produced working with Ensor Holiday and Keith Laws, and developing one in particular which gave a geometric pattern compatible with both a delicate single layer stainless steel structure and the current capacity of the glass industry to produce doubly curved laminated glass panels to acceptable tolerances. Translating the characteristics of beauty of a natural pearl into a glass sphere at a scale four to five thousand times larger was also a challenge. We interpreted these in the twenty-metre diameter sphere through:
– sphericity: smooth surface, absence of visible fixings, discreteness of joints, fabrication, construction and thermal movement tolerances
– translucency: choice of both glasses, interlayer and surface treatment
– lustre/depth: choice of glass, thickness, coatings and surface treatment
– iridescence: optical/surface qualities of outer glass sheet (day), internal central lighting system performance (night).

It was important that the external aesthetic of the pearl was not compromised by the legibility of the structure during the day, and that, when illuminated internally from a radial light source at night, it did not cast rogue shadows on the inner surface of the glass. To avoid any material, other than glass, visible on the external surface, we designed and tested a prototype countersunk articulated fixing which allowed the external glass surface to be laminated across it. We named it the 'phantom' fixing. Collaborating with TW Ide in London, prototypes of doubly curved glass pentagon and triangular panels were made; and with Produits Sully in France, prototype glass fixing assemblies were load tested to convince ourselves and our client of the feasibility of the

Above: Main suspension fixing, La Villette Museum; Detail of glass cladding, B8 building, Stockley Park; *Centre*: Model of Pearl of the Gulf, Dubai and three-dimensional glass panel sample; *Below*: Glass seat and wall supports, Bermondsey Station, Jubilee Line Extension

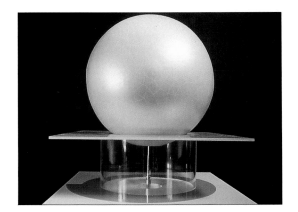

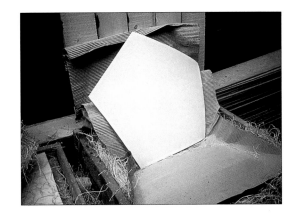

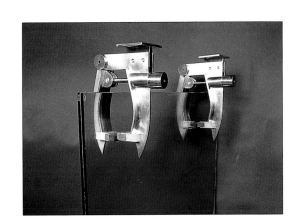

project. As with the facades at La Villette, the behaviour of the structure in relation to the glass skin was crucial and we designed the glass fixing assembly incorporating spring mountings – to overcome construction tolerances, differential thermal movement and structural deformation between the structure and the glass skin.

Through the development of new technologies, our own architecture will become more dynamic and less material, in the sense that transparent structural materials such as glass and diamond films will become the support medium for holograms, miniaturised lasers and biogenetic coatings offering the possibilities to improve energy efficiency, to create interactive building surfaces to both user and the environment and release new creative energies in the design and visual pleasure of our buildings.

(*Ian Ritchie*, Royal Institution Lecture, *Oct 1992*)

Yet if we stop to think, we realise that we have accepted a departure of many bodies in the late 20th century: a software-monitored society, a world of infrastructures, bleeps and wafer thin calculators, all of them suggesting that the world of the touchable, recognisable moving-part is receding. Yet design is still at pains to reassure us that it should all look 'like something' and in parallel there is a certain morality that suggests that architectural objects should have a solid sense of purpose allied to a solid sense of presence. In other words, architecture is a slow-witted and conservative art and this bridge (Lintas Bridge, Paris) is a somewhat illegitimate object. Yet it has not always been so . . . Plate glass in particular became the dream-as-reality material of the 20th century. 'It's there – but it's not there' seems to suggest the same adrenalin buzz as surfing or flying.

(*Peter Cook*, Blueprint, *May 1987*)

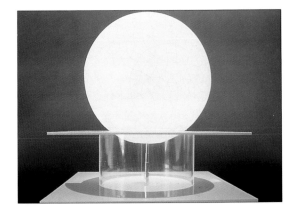

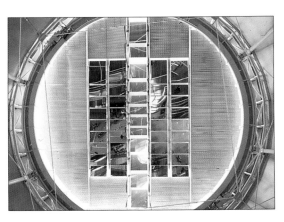

From above: Model of Pearl of the Gulf at night; Mirror mock-up for La Villette Museum; Bermondsey Station model; Computer controlled mylar mirrors of La Villette's rotating domes to control sun's rays; *Opposite*: Lintas Bridge at night

HUMAN PURPOSE

Architecture and economics

Is there a cost penalty for design by architects? It would appear that most people who commission buildings believe there is, since the number of buildings, certainly in the UK, which are designed by a commissioned architect represents only the tip of the iceberg of our built environment.

To most people who finance our built environment it would appear that design is intangible, and of insignificant or no benefit, and that if you have 'design' it costs more than if you don't have it, and why pay up front for something which is intangible?

As architects, it is important that we recognise that this is a current reality, certainly in the UK, and that architects are probably viewed as a luxury by most people who perceive our recent contribution to the urban environment as very poor. Clearly there is now a recognised need for a missionary endeavour by architects and their professional institution to change this perception through a public and school education programme, by debate, and by raising architectural quality.

Our experience has given us a belief and delight in simplicity and economy as a design aim, and that they are inseparable ingredients in realising architecture. Economy has validity even when we are at the earliest stages of imagining concepts.

Clients vary enormously in their appreciation and communication of the financial constraints of their projects. This requires us to be particularly attuned to cost issues at a strategic level as well as at the more detailed level of building costs, from both our perception of the client's viewpoint as well as our own. There are those clients in the commercial sector such as Stanhope, for whom we designed the B8 building at Stockley Park, who, with their cost consultants, were extremely rigorous from the outset in expressing the financial framework in

Right: B8 Building, Stockley Park, Heathrow; Concept layout of Spitalfields Gardens, London; Roy Square Housing, London

relation to a very clear brief and what they expected of the architect. Most importantly this framework remained constant throughout the project. To achieve an architecture from these tight constraints we conceived a tactic to establish mutual confidence by demonstrating our industrial credibility. This was achieved within the first few weeks of the relationship by producing a generic enclosure design, with a notional surface area, and having industry confirm its willingness to commit to a guaranteed maximum price (GMP) for a specified period beyond the anticipated completion date for the building (at this early stage there was no agreed design footprint for the building).

On the other hand, there are those clients who were vague, or completely inexperienced and with whom, by demonstrating commitment, mutual confidence and trust became the most important mechanism in managing the economy of the project, (even to the extent, on occasions of personally constructing the buildings).

We have initiated different methods of balancing architecture and economy at various stages of a project's development. For example, by immediately, and somewhat audaciously, challenging the brief fundamentally, as at Elder Gardens, Spitalfields. This involved questioning and independently checking the viability of developing luxury apartments in the context of the overall economics of the entire development, and consequently proposing the potential financial, urban design and political advantages to our client of a new London Square, which could ultimately provide social and amenity benefits for both the existing local neighbourhood and the new business community. This strategy was accepted by our client, even though it represented a huge reduction in our potential fee income! At Hermitage Riverside and Roy Square, we instigated a significant increase in the density and number of apart-ments on the site (more with less) in order to make the development more financially viable, and architecturally much more satisfactory in relation to the scale of their respective immediate environments, the River Thames and Limehouse Basin/Narrow Street.

Almost inevitably, as the design process evolves, the initial framework and controls established at the outset are tested. This has convinced us of the importance of ensuring that they are well thought through and appropriate to the client and the envisaged project seen in its wider context.

The seminal project which best illustrates our anticipation of the need to have a framework and control beyond the habitual, was the Albert Cultural Centre. We recognised the limited experience of the municipality and we were familiar with the traditional contractual methods, programming, role and the performance of French trade contractors on public contracts. Having won an open competition, we anticipated being seen as 'innocent foreigners' by local contractors. Given this scenario, and our own genuine concern to see the project built on time, to cost and to the detail quality we believed possible, together with our psychological and financial limitations inherited from the conventional fee and contractual obligation structure in France, we were led to propose and finally undertake for the first time in France on a public contract, construction management, including the cost control during construction phase to completion. This enabled us to have not only the construction and programming expertise early on in the project but also allowed us to establish continuity through our permanent on-site presence. We managed to meet the target programme, costs, (under budget) and quality (despite two major contractors, structural steelwork and metalwork, passing into receivership at critical moments during construction).

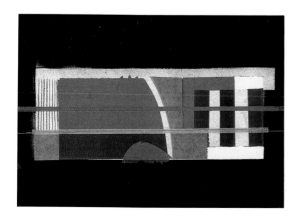

Compliance, conflict and reason

The design process seeks the fundamentals of a problem, often redefining them. Questioning traditional solutions, preconceived ideas, the client's practices and even the need to build at all, is a challenge for both client and architect. It is nevertheless necessary to achieve an optimum solution whether it is innovative or not.

On the architect's side, this process, the newly acquired knowledge of the problems and opportunities specific to the project are constantly checked against the architect's professional conscience on the basis of his/her experience and moral values There may be problems in this process. The values of the client may be diametrically opposed to those of the architect. Whereas the law provides a certain framework within which to work, and certain recognisable boundaries which a professional should not transgress for any client, there will be other territories which the architect, as a person, would keep away from. If the values and moral integrity of the architect are unclear, these territories will be more difficult to identify, and vary among team-members.

In 1989, we were commissioned by Olympia + York to design the first speculative office building at Heron Quays, as part of phase three of the Canary Wharf development. Being unconvinced by the master plan for this phase of three million square feet, we expressed our considered views on its shortcomings to the client and the other consultants. Our views questioned the inadequacies of the ground level public domain, the interface with future infrastructures and other strategic issues, which, without further resolution, not only inhibited an intelligent approach to the design of the particular building but affected the viability of the proposals. After visiting New York on two separate occasions to resolve our differences with the master planners, it remained clear that our continued questioning was necessary. This was unacceptable to the client, and in a last effort to clarify our concerns we prepared a new master plan in April 1990 and mailed it directly to Olympia + York in Toronto. Within weeks the proposals for phase three were shelved, indefinitely. Canary Wharf collapsed financially in 1992.

It is clear that there are non-legal but moral limits to what an architect will do for a client. If the architect were to put these personal limits aside in a supposed 'favour' to a client, or for personal benefit, then the architect would not only compromise personal integrity, but also the quality of the end product and therefore the quality of the service being offered to the client in the first place. In such a situation there must be the option for either party to decide to terminate the relationship.

The known and unknown user

Whereas the client should normally have at least the interest of the known users at heart, it is often up to the architect to represent the unknown users. Sometimes even vital interests of the known users are ignored by a client in favour of subjective self-interest.

In the absence of the client's conscious acceptance of a more holistic responsibility, the architect has to take up the cause of the passer-by, the neighbour, the long-term view, the environment etc.

We believe that the inclusion of these social and wider economic concerns in the thought process ought to be to the advantage of the client and user in the longer term. The product will be a better building and this will be recognised, if not by the client initially, then maybe by the employees, visitors, competitors, or bankers or someone else who needs to appreciate other qualities in the building.

Of course to presume a better knowledge of a client's interest than the client himself suggests an arrogance, but it may just be a different knowledge, a different aspect

From above: Conceptual views, Heron Quays, London: along north edge of quay; within Heron Square; within office entrance court; towards the South Garden

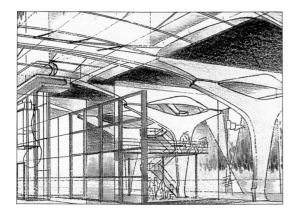

of the client's intention that complements what the client wants from the collaboration with the architect.

The most difficult projects are those where the user is less well defined, such as speculative office buildings. The temptation for the client to follow a well rehearsed formula, and to instruct his architect accordingly, leaves little scope for anticipating future user patterns, behaviour and desires. Unless one can achieve a significant degree of confidence with the client and his property advisory, to at least open discussions about the future and holistic issues, the architect's concerns can never reach a stage of credibility.

An interesting experience was the building services concept for such a building at Oxford Science Park, where our desire for a naturally ventilated building went against the standard formula of air conditioned space. However, with confidence and open reasoned discussion between the client, the funders, the letting agents, services and structural engineers, quantity surveyors and ourselves, a strategy was agreed for a naturally ventilated building, with the future potential for zoned or full floor air conditioning.

FUNCTION

Form follows desire

With very few exceptions, the forms and their composition that we have created have more to do with desire than with function.

In some projects, such as the Pearl of the Gulf and the Meridian Planetarium, the form is symbolic. Eagle Rock is a sculptural expression of a client's desire, and like the Fluy House visually subdues the passive solar energy aspect. The Boves Pharmacy is a sculptural expression of our desires, licensed by the site context, where the main road has an extraordinary collection of different building forms, scales and materials. Our proposition for a new National Maritime Museum of the Boat was informed by a desire to complete the celebrated classical architectural composition of the Greenwich Waterfront with the 'auditorium and orchestra pit' across the River Thames, in a manner that was more landscape than building, inspired by some works of conceptual land artists, such as Robert Smithson. The Thames would then become the stage, Wren's Naval College and Inigo Jones' Queen's House the stage set, and the Greenwich Observatory the 'fly tower'. The La Villette facades represented a desire to define transparency, once this concept was established, and also a desire to make legible how they worked.

At a smaller scale within the design we attempted to express a clear understanding between the form and forces in the structural elements from which they were made, hence the choice of the spring suspension and cables to give clear form to the tension forces. Functionally, the two glass walls and the bridges which cross the chasm of the Ecology Gallery at the Natural History Museum, could in themselves have been much simpler. However the underlying preconcept of a fragile environment, here described simply as earth, air, fire and water, informed a desire to represent the elements through

From above: 'Dolphin' suspension arm, Reina Sofia Museum of Modern Art, Madrid; Detail of *Guernica*, Pablo Picasso, 1937, MOMA, New York; Scheme for B8 Building, Stockley Park, Heathrow; B8 Building as constructed

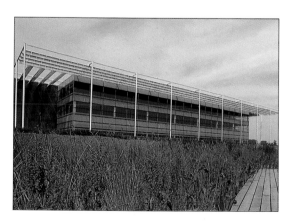

straight and curved forms and light; an asymmetrical spatial composition which makes reference to the apparent natural state of disequilibrium. The deliberately crude and heavy design of the bridges, together with the suggested sophistication expressed by their doubly curved form, and the finesse of only some components, was intended to symbolise man and his current relationship with the earth. The form of the 'dolphin' suspension arms holding the glass sheets at Reina Sophia derives its angle to the glass from our desire to permanently express their suspension under different temperature conditions. The resultant curvilinear profile 'captures' the outstretched arm holding the lamp (future) in Picasso's *Guernica*.

An exception is the B8 office/research facility at Stockley Park. An initial desire to allow the landscape and skyscape visually to dissolve the building, led us to a simple curved form. This form would always create a tangential view of the roof against the sky, and allow the landscape to invade the curved edges formed by the structure bringing landscape to skyscape. The rectangular form of the built design is by comparison conventional, yet by stripping the building envelope to a bare minimum, its functional brief is given a new architectural identity.

Ian Ritchie's building was, without doubt, the most aesthetically refined of any of the buildings that we saw this year. It is also the most poetic response to the banal commercial formulae that the developers of Stockley Park impose on their architects. By cleaving to the formula, as if to a sacred text, it reveals its spiritual, its intellectual emptiness. But that is the devastating effect of all real art, to tell the truth about its subject. The question that the critics, and the panel face, before the essentially tragic application of such a poetic intensity to such banal intentions, is, does one award the singer, or the song?
(*John Outram, assessor, FT Awards Publication, 1991*)

When Brancusi explored the form of the egg to derive simple expressions of life, it would appear that his desire was to capture this life in new forms, representing both embryo and adult. His sleeping head, lying on a cushion, with the faint lines of closed eyes is very different from his bird in space, yet both derive from the same 'original' egg form. The metals come to life in light, their contours belonging only to the form itself, which is neither engineered, nor utilitarian, but felt. In architecture, accommodating people and their utilitarian needs and the engineering of forces, requires a level of understanding and sophistication even to imagine creating forms so beautiful as those sculptures. Equally, the handling of material on a much larger scale can so easily begin to undermine simplicity and economy. If, as in the case of structural engineering (eg a telecommunications mast) there is the potential to derive beauty simply from the profile and the chosen material, excessive structural gymnastics, expressions of style or decoration, simply camouflage and destroy the potential beauty of form.

'I do not think that architecture can be an art. For me art is not functional and is without everyday value' (*Richard Serra interview, Bern 1990*)

In Leipzig, through the invitation of von Gerkan, Marg and Partners, we have sought, using glass, to find simplicity and economy through form for the enormous reception halls, exploring various radii and the extent of cylindrical surfaces; and whether the purity of form will be best perceived from within the glass halls or from without. From these studies of form, material and the engineering of them, we can begin to define the relationship of the structure to glass skin in such a way as to ensure that the form, perceived in different lighting conditions will hold visual centre stage, without eclipsing the aesthetic role of the engineering in the compositional hierarchy of the architecture in its landscape setting.

In our architecture, we do not describe a form and then force the utilitarian needs and its engineering to distort or contort itself in order to achieve it.

Form, structure, energy and materials are all in the crucible together, and our desire is to melt these into a whole composition where changing light can unlock the secret of the form, within and without, of the architecture.

Visual mathematics, using computers, offers us real possibilities to describe new forms, three dimensional surfaces and volumes, which hitherto, have been essentially limited to the platonic solids and sliced geometric games of solid and void with them.

More from less

In searching for economy, there is the real chance of producing a poetic response. A response which can express and reveal our search for economy, by providing more from less.

The Fluy House, almost devoid of expressive details, gives this impression, yet the spatial generosity camouflages the low construction budget (£30,000 in 1976). The structure of thin walled hollow steel sections weighs only 12.5 kilogrammes/square metres, and the glass skinned walls and highly insulated roof enclose a ground plan area of 245 square metres; added to which is an internal basement of 36 square metres and a 40-square-metre cellar in the earth for wine and solar energy storage, and space to grow mushrooms.

The feeling of spaciousness is achieved by the high degree of transparency and flow of the internal spaces. Yet, from the landscaped garden the house appears small and reticent. Consequently, the small corner site appears much larger and within the landscape there are spaces where the house cannot be seen at all.

The Reina Sofia circulation towers used flat elements for the structure, glass and stainless steel components,

Opposite: Glass walls and bridges of the Ecology Gallery, Natural History Museum, London

inspired by the black, grey and white 'collage' impression of Picasso's *Guernica*, (which 'defines' the beginning of the museum's modern art permanent collection), revealing simplicity and economy of material, yet combined in the overall composition, created a visual richness and complexity.

The lightness of these towers is largely achieved by allowing the glass panels at the corners to transfer the wind loads around the corners. The main glass suspension 'dolphin's' profile form uses the minimum amount of stainless steel plate to engage the suspension rod assemblies and the structural loads.

Lintas Bridge, designed in 1985, and the La Villette facades of the same period, are the most expressive of our architectures where we have captured the notion of 'more from less'. The Lintas Bridge, however, does not reveal why it is a glass bridge or why it is a minimum all glass box suspended from a lightweight prestressed structure. Concealed below there is an existing blacked out glazed dome, which could not be touched, hence the bridge. The ephemeral qualities, as well as the virtual ceiling created at night across the courtyard by reflections of light between the glass walls of the bridge, sought to give a contemporary commentary on our advertising agency client.

What makes the bridge important rather than just naughty is its tautness of manner, its very economy of means: for example, the ways in which the pieces of glass are just clipped into place, the lighting held by wires, the whole thing wired-up with the sort of relaxed style that we are familiar with in hi-fi or camping but seem to get screwed-up over when making a building. Philosophically, it gives just the very jolt that is much needed in the field of design. The fact that it feels as if it might fracture – aesthetically – but that it is not likely to – technically –

introduces its ambience very well. Somehow a comment is being made upon the 'edgy', the 'real/unreal' world of advertising, by a similarly edgy, real/unreal piece of architecture.
(*Peter Cook*, Blueprint, *May 1987*)

Our proposal for the Meridian Planetarium at Greenwich is spherical, for symbolic reasons. Inside, however, we have imagined the starfields projected over the entire inner surface of the sphere, enabling both the southern and northern hemispherical skies to be projected simultaneously. We have called it a spheriscope. Not only does this increase the experience of the visitor but it gives some rationale beyond the symbolism of the sphere. The architectural form is a minimum surface volume, whose outer skin of glass can also be illuminated, revealing the paths of satellites and creating a modern navigation and communication reference to our planet.

Use and beauty
Can function be a source of art?

Beauty is a by-product of art when there is pleasure derived from it. Art is extracting an essence and translating it.

Man seeks security, thus security is a function whether physical or spiritual. Man seeks shelter, thus shelter is a function. If we consider shelter, it can be provided by walls (from the wind), by a roof on columns, (from rain and sun), and by a roof on walls (from rain, sun and wind).

If we take a column, the function of which is to support a roof, and look at a metaphor in nature – the tree trunk (bypassing early Mediterranean timber architecture, the later stone architecture which apparently represented timber construction, and all the other historical references as well), we can maybe rediscover the present. Our present day ability to evoke the tree trunk, if we choose it as the familiar model for a column, gives us the

Above: Fluy House, Picardy, France; *Centre*: Reina Sofia Museum of Modern Art, Madrid; Ecology Gallery glass bridge, with leaf patterns of ginko biloba and horse chestnut; *Below*: Conceptual interior of Meridian Planetarium, Greenwich with the world's first 360-degree view of the stars, both northern and southern hemisphere, and transparent plane in centre of sphere for the 'floating' audience; Proposed riverside view from Royal Naval College

opportunity to understand the beauty of a tree afresh, and to 'extract' the essential elements of it, be they visual, mathematical or technical. This should enable us to imagine, create or invent a functional form from our perception and from our scientific understanding of it. We then search for a representation of the support which raises the support function to that of potential beauty.

Our artistic expression is not only informed by our perception of the tree, but also from the material we choose, the scientific understanding we have of that material, and what the column is supporting and the load it will carry. Let us assume we choose glass, because this is consistent with, say, our preconcept (eg, the tree is symbolic of our fragile coexistence with the planet) and concept (eg, an ephemeral architecture for an Information Age Company). Glass can be very strong in compression, but also in tension – in the form of woven glass fibres. Glass is also perceived by most people as fragile. We have a link – fragility – between the material and the preconcept, and glass is also recognised as being and not being present – ephemeral, providing a reference to the concept. In the form of a column, woven glass fibres do not immediately suggest either fragility or compression, yet as a composite, no doubt one could make them work physically. However, the potential to reveal the ephemeral qualities of the concept would be very difficult to achieve. A transparent glass column would, on the other hand evoke strong emotions, both of fragility and ephemerality. Both of the above columns would demonstrate a contemporary understanding of glass as a material, and could be developed in a form which would demonstrate the technology of glass production in our age.

The foregoing hypothetical example raises the simple question – why bother to go to the apparent extreme of designing a glass column in the first place? Stone, timber, steel, concrete and bricks are all available and are good in compression.

We believe we should bother and we should search. This is man's natural instinct – to search for understanding, and consequently change and the new. But it must be relevant and it must have meaning.

In the above example the meaning is derived from our present concerns for the environment, the symbolic importance of the tree, the tree trunk as a natural model of support, and the transience of the information age. Our imagination creates, from this, the glass column, and our skill as designers should reveal its essence.

There are many examples of these functions in architecture that come to mind.

Art is expressed in these buildings, in its essence, through a perceptive imitation of nature, eg, the shells of Sydney Opera House, or of an architectural predecessor, eg, Pavilion of the Future's stone arcade, Seville.

It can also be expressed subversively – as an instigator of change, eg Centre Pompidou, which changed our perception of high cultural architecture by demonstrably removing the 'entrance steps'.

Subversive statements tend to create a painful emotional response initially, rather than one of pleasure, which is why subversion and beauty are difficult companions.

The application of science is seen in many countries as subversive because its very nature is progressive.

Every work of art is the child of its age and, in many cases, the mother of our emotions. It follows that each period of culture produces an art of its own which can never be repeated. Efforts to revive the art-principles of the past will at best produce an art that is still-born. it is impossible for us to live and feel, as did the ancient Greeks.

(*Kandinsky*, Concerning the Spiritual in Art, *1911*)

Opposite: Lintas Bridge, Paris (photograph, Alain Guisdard)

CONSTRUCTION

Triangle of confidence

There have been several references to confidence in the preceding pages. There is little doubt from our experience that this is one of the most important characteristics which is finally reflected in the built architecture.

We believe it is absolutely necessary to establish a principal triangle of confidence between the client, the design team and industry. Without it the project will suffer. It is the lines of communication between the three parties, each of whom may individually have confidence, which transmit this confidence.

Projects are realised as a collaborative venture, and the more open the relationships the better the communication. Although contracts are an inevitable part of the collaborative framework, their importance to us lies in their value in communicating what each party is expected to contribute to in the project. Once this has been established they should simply represent a 'safety net', which is only useful when something goes seriously wrong, usually resulting from a lack of communication.

If the lines of communication become weak and risk breaking, we use our utmost endeavours to reinforce them. However, if one of them should break and be irreplaceable, then knowing that the project will not become what was imagined, we have on occasions preferred to withdraw from the project.

There are many pleasures in architecture, but one of them is certainly not living nightmares without a supportive framework based on the triangle of confidence.

Problems inevitably arise, yet they can be a source of a great deal of pleasure through solving them, providing that this triangle of confidence exists. It is not uncommon that problems highlight commitment, and we have rarely experienced the 'rabbit phenomena' at the moment problems are identified, when everyone suddenly disappears.

Right: Pharmacy, Boves, France; Planning permission model of Eagle Rock; Mock-up of Louvre Pyramid (photograph, RFR)

Skills

Architecture's richness and diversity is such that it often seems that there is insufficient time available to practise all the necessary skills, in order to gain and create confidence, with humility.

One mechanism we employ is the training and learning on small projects. This provides us with an opportunity for the less practised architects in our office to lead a project within a framework of mutual support, and collectively to explore ideas, materials and techniques in the knowledge that the research, application and evaluation will be realised relatively quickly. These projects, more often than not, have no financial benefit to the office in isolation, but do engender a spirit of recognising the equal importance of all projects and their particular value in the development of skills and our architecture. They are very often the source of first practice by a young architect in the whole process, dealing with real opportunities and problems (managing nightmares), and as such are invaluable in the longer term. In the short term they provide excellent 'object lessons' in what not to do, as much as what to do for all of us.

In our studio, the conventional exploratory skills of drawing, model-making and using CAD are developed and supported only when there is individual motivation. We do not have in-house computing, model-making or graphic presentation specialists. Each person has to take responsibility for developing their own skills and best method of working, and in this way nobody becomes pigeon-holed. Everyone serves everyone else to the best of their abilities. Practise, practise and practise is in the end the only real way to achieve the level of skills required to have any chance of realising, with satisfaction, dreams and aspirations, and without real clients the process of architecture is curtailed and many skills remain undeveloped.

Nuts and bolts

Fundamental to our concern with the way things are put together is the desire to understand the nature of the materials and how they can be manipulated. This understanding is not only intellectual, but unites head and hand. Many schools of architecture subject their students to technical lecture courses in structural analysis and material properties (not bad things, in themselves). The materials are often not seen, handled or worked with. The structural analysis is sometimes 'supported' with the making of little models. Nothing could be more deceptive. Paper might be a reasonable representation of concrete or steel at a scale of 1:1000, but only within strictly defined parameters and with dramatically varying scaling factors. An intuitive understanding of structures, built at full size, is an invaluable support to design and structural analysis.

There is a preponderance of people in the office who have personally constructed full-sized structures, many of them highly speculative, experimental, and some of them certainly not justifiable by conventional engineering standards. Similarly, in the course of most projects, visits and close discussions with fabricators are an essential part of the early design process. Whenever possible (almost without exception), we involve fabricators long before any contract can be awarded. Here, as with consultants, such as materials scientists, we are fortunate in having established a very supportive network of experts, (metals, glass, light, fabrics, aggregates etc) and through mutual respect their input leads to important developments and refinement of the design. The design process is also aided by the making of full size mock-ups and prototypes. These serve not only to help us make aesthetic decisions, but also to test the ease of assembly, of replacement and to use them as confirmation of theoretical analysis.

When detailing certain components, especially for prototypes, such as those requiring machining and threading, these are described at scales greater than full size, eg 5:1. This can also help establish mutual respect between those involved, by demonstrating our interest and level of understanding of materials and techniques.

There is a delicate balance to be struck between our instincts to be sculptors, freely moulding and manipulating materials, enjoying perhaps some of their more perverse intrinsic properties (corrosion, rough cast surfaces, for example), and tempering these desires with a feeling of responsibility to our client and to practical good sense.

Relationships and reality with industry

The importance of a good working relationship with industry is vital to the excellent realisation of architectural ideas. One can find within the construction industry information, skill and energy, which, if available during the early design stages can enhance rather than curtail ideas, by challenging the architect to express intentions even more clearly. We have described how we seek to collaborate with industry in evaluating options and prototypes, and why, in the section on materials. But this is not all.

How do we initiate and establish these links and foster them? Through motivation and enthusiasm tempered by an understanding of how industry can help, and by being as clear and specific as possible from the outset. One's attitude should not be arrogant or indeed limit the space in which the particular industrial advice and collaboration is being sought. Equally, if an idea is germinating then it can be useful to explore with industry where the material, fabrication or construction limits may lie, without necessarily accepting these limits as finite. The processing factory or production works are typically a source of discovery and ideas for us, where the essence and qualities of materials can be better perceived by us. It is obviously much easier to practise this within the context of a real project with enlightened clients willing to fund research during projects, and where industry can recognise a tangible involvement and potential benefit. However, one must remain aware of the possibility of one's own preconceived notions inhibiting an open exploration with industry. When the context is without an immediate application, ie research and development, the ability for an architect to involve, motivate and obtain the support of industry is much more difficult. This confirms the distinct difference between the more ideological aspects of architecture and the profit motive of industry, despite their symbiotic relationship.

The initial contact on Reina Sofia came from the Spanish general contractor, not the client (Ministry of Culture), nor the architects appointed to transform the hospital building into a museum of modern art. The 'reality' sought by the contractor was the certainty of a buildable solution within a very severe time constraint, to the problem of moving visitors and goods vertically. They saw the RFR design of the La Villette facades as the enclosure solution to the circulation towers, however we did not. The 'challenge' they put to us was a contractual proposition that if we failed to produce a design which met the requirements of their 'reality', ie that any new design we produced could be made and erected by the glass industry, then we would receive no fees! We accepted, not on the principle of their proposition, but in order to establish confidence and trust between us.

The ability to understand and to accept others' terms of reference, not innocently, and to measure them against our own assessment of our capabilities without inflating either is, I believe, always part of the 'engagement' equation; and if, as in the case of Reina Sofia, confidence

From above: Glass and stainless steel circulation tower, Reina Sofia Museum of Modern Art, Madrid; Detail of the tower's structural components; Side view of bioclimatic facade, La Villette Museum

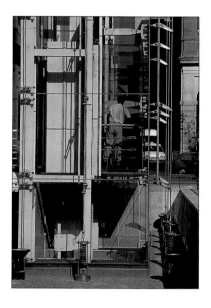

and trust is established so early on, then mutual respect should follow and bode well for our involvement and the outcome of the project.

A more recent example was in France, in realising the Cultural Centre, Albert. Having identified the need for management control ('Architecture and economics', Human Purpose, p63), the next step was to convince the mayor, councillors and their project operations advisors, the Direction Departmental d'Equipement (DDE) of the Somme. We, as a design team, first needed to establish a level of confidence with them prior to any presentation jointly with Schal International of the principles and potential advantages of construction management (CM), although Schal had been assisting us since our competition win. The presentation was followed by their visit to Stockley Park and the B8 building to illustrate the results of our previous collaboration with Schal, and also to discuss the importance of the client's ability to be clear and decisive. During this visit we discussed the need for a clear communications structure between the client and ourselves and how Schal could help facilitate this in respect of the construction operations. Subsequently, a special grant was made available by the French Government, secured by the DDE, to finance a slightly abridged form of CM and for it to be monitored and evaluated on this project. Although the client/CM contract was signed with us, rather than with Schal, it was done so in the open knowledge by all involved that Schal would be contributing their construction management expertise on behalf of the client.

The six months available between our engagement and the required opening deadline, coupled with the very limited cost and fee allowance for the Boves Pharmacy precipitated the involvement of Viry s.a. This steelwork fabricator, based in Epinal, south-east France, had previously constructed the entrance hall roof and the

Park Galleries at La Villette, and were at the time involved in fabricating the 'cloud' at the Grand Arch, all to RFR designs. There existed an understanding and trust between us. Our request that Viry confirm acceptance of the programme and our cost estimate for the frame, floors, walls and enclosure of the building based on our outline sketch design was confirmed within a few days. The project was then undertaken between us only by telecommunication (fax and phone), covering the detail design and shop drawings. Site preparation works and services installations were co-ordinated by fax through an architect's office in Amiens, and client communications via a fax in the village. Only when the building was delivered by wide load trucks at the beginning of June 1990 did we see the results and limitations of telecommunicating with the contractor.

This revealed certain unexpected cultural differences; in particular, that we treated faxes as a substitute for round table discussions during the early design stages, whereas the contractor took them as if they were letters, leading to 'formalities' and unnecessary delays. Also, in the knowledge that we would not be inspecting the works prior to delivery and erection, nor arriving in Epinal to put 'eyeball' pressure on Viry to meet the programme, the contractor took some small liberties in the fabricated details and gave us some anxiety over the programme. Overall the outcome was successful, however with a less well established relationship this may have proved far more serious.

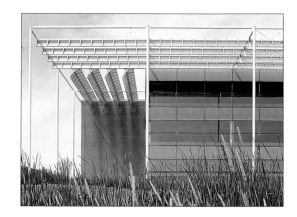

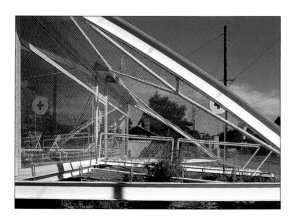

From above: **B8 Building, Stockley Park, Heathrow**; **Aerial view of B8 Building**; **Pharmacy, Boves, France**; *Opposite*: **Cultural Centre, Albert, France**

AUTHENTICITY IN ARCHITECTURE

Head, heart and hands

The contents of the book, so far, should have given a good insight into the way we approach projects, and how we undertake them. What should be apparent is that architecture and landscape is made by people for people, and is not about individual egos.

Client, designer and industry have to collaborate, and in doing so bring to the project their strengths and weaknesses, their intellect, their emotions and their physical skills. In summary, head, heart and hands.

The process of creating architecture, with its rich diversity of people, cannot escape the effects of this combination, and in fact benefits from it. However, it is so important to recognise when and how these individual characteristics are most appropriately engaged on the project. It is never the same, but one's awareness should always be highly tuned to the opportunities they offer to enrich not only the architecture but also the pleasure in the process.

Often, the heart is the least consideration, yet it is our belief that the spirit captured in the built architecture reveals this aspect more than any other. One can often enter a contemporary building and feel whether the process of realising it was enjoyed by those who created it, whereas entering an historical building is conditioned to a large extent by received 'knowledge' of the social and cultural context of its time.

We described in concepts the potential energy store that a concept can provide, which, coupled with the openness and generosity of the people involved, creates the pleasure and enjoyment, which is measured by the heart. This is the pleasure which becomes enshrined in the finished building, to be appreciated and enjoyed by all who use it.

When you can feel in your heart that something is right, this is partly where the beauty comes from.

Above: Interior perspective, Natural History Museum, London; *Right*: Interior of Eagle Rock under construction; Computer simulation of structure, Leipzig Messe Glass Halls (with GMP), Germany; Lintas Bridge, Paris

Art, science and construction for human purpose

Architecture is the art, science and construction for human purpose, and must reveal humanity: a humanity which is apparent in its component design, its overall composition and the manner in which it is constructed and placed within the existing whole environment.

Our attitude to architecture is one that does not demand that we shriek through design extremism to appeal to the media, or seek the hyper-mediatisation of our projects. There is too much 'shrieking' in society.

Although Western society at many levels is still on the crest of egomania, there is an earth which constantly reminds us of the consequences of the selfishness of man. Today there is a need to share architecture that lifts our emotions and spirit by the manipulation of light, space, use of materials and composition, but also through the manner and conduct with which we execute it. Simply bringing people together to work collectively with aims beyond personal interest is surely one of the most significant arts one can perform – architecture is a wonderful arena.

Ideas and the quality of them, sometimes audacious, inspire those with whom we work and are fundamental to the development and realisation of architecture. They occur in the minds of individuals as a result of discussing preconcepts, and are explored and tested at the conceptual stage across the spectrum of architectural issues. Those ideas which survive, nourish and frame the entire design process, which, with the quality and thoroughness of research and application inevitably produce architecture of real meaning and experience.

Practising architecture at the end of the 20th century requires us to restate that it is a synthetic process. Its material foundation has for the last few centuries been knowledge established largely through reductionist science. This knowledge base is beginning to shift.

Chaos theory and the science of complexity explored through computer simulation indicate how matter and life itself apparently synthesise from simple elements into simple systems with complex organisational and behavioural characteristics. This is a conceptual way of thinking that builds up rather than breaks down, recognising interdependence rather than independence in much the same way that we seek to produce our architecture.

This is the process of architecture we enjoy

> . . . one wonders whether these 'creative' minds realise that architecture can, once in a while, be as audacious as they?

(*Peter Cook*, Blueprint, *May 1987, referring to the Lintas Bridge, Paris*)

In his last lecture, less than a year before he died, John Constable (1776-1837) put his objections to the Gothic revival:

> A new gothic building . . . is in reality little less absurd than a new ruin . . . it is to be lamented that the tendency of taste is at present too much toward this kind of imitation, which, as long as it lasts, can only act as blight on art, by engaging talents that might have stamped the Age with a character of its own, in the vain endeavour to re-animate deceased Art, in which the utmost which can be accomplished will be to reproduce a body without a soul.

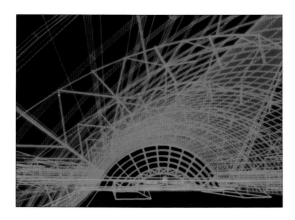

HERNE-SODINGEN ACADEMY, GERMANY

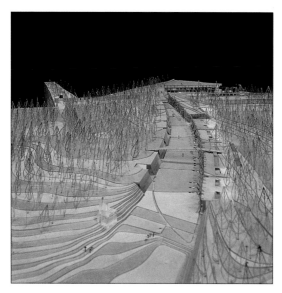

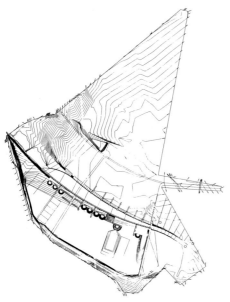

Above: Model of the site, looking from the north-west

If you want to plan a year ahead,
plant a tree
If you want to plan ten years ahead,
sow a seed
If you want to plan one hundred years ahead,
educate the people.
Kuan Tzu (Chinese poet) 500BC

The preconcept for the Herne-Sodingen Academy Park is an intellectual and moral statement which subsequently informs the architectural concept and its physical interpretation. Education is at the heart of this project, both in terms of primary function (Academy) and desire (ecology). Education is the need to be aware, understand and appreciate. In an ecological sense (ecology: *oikos* (Gr) house or dwelling – as the word 'economy') this is the appreciation of the beauty and value of species, and the realisation of the need to act to avoid despoliation and the dying out of our living companions on earth.

In order to act sensibly, and do good, we need to understand how the planet works, and how its species survive. Appreciation comes from awareness, sensible action comes from knowledge, knowledge comes from science and research, and technique comes through strategic policy makers; policies to enable correct action come from government. One function of science is to help and control the world we live in; the other, which is more important, is simply to help us appreciate it. This appreciation changes our attitudes for the better. It is this preconcept which drives the definition of an architectural concept for the Academy project.

The reclamation of the landscape forms a central theme to both the overall planning for the IBA Emscher Park region, and to the specific desires for the Herne-Sodingen Academy Park. If high environmental expectations are to be realised for the Academy buildings, even more must be expected of the wider landscape into which they are to be integrated.

Landscape can and should be much more than a visual amenity. It can function on many interacting levels, central to which is the restoration of a meaningful contact with the natural world. Its benefits can have a widespread social and economic value, indicating and suggesting the wise use of materials, natural energy and manpower resources. Such an approach will go a long way to help compensate for an environment that has suffered from the ill effects of industrial usage and exploitation. To achieve a social landscape, observing intelligent ecological principles, will require changes in attitude (already indicated by the client's brief) of society, in the administration of open space management, and in the education of those who will become, in the future, responsible for its planning and design.

There is a growing acceptance of such ideas in Europe, and the educational opportunity offered by this site is very important if natural landscape restoration principles are to be understood and act as a catalyst for further development in the large environment of Emscher Park.

The Herne-Sodingen Academy Park is to be an Educational Woodland Park, available to all sections of the community, as well as the Academy. The primary succession by which an area of barren ground is colonised by a series of plant regimes, reflects, in the space of just a few decades, a whole story of plant evolution through to a mature woodland community. It is this simple idea which had determined the architect's concept for the land as an evolutionary woodland park. It is also a statement about time and our appreciation of 'the relative speed of change'. The successful implementation of the woodland park will require the active participation of the local town community and school children in concert with the public authorities. To be a participant means access to knowledge and awareness of the proposals and to the process and time of its implementation.

Outside of the Academy's specific curriculum, the park will provide a diverse range of learning opportunities from the more formal, such as the scientific research and study of the soil and natural habitat, to the informal, such as children's play. These educational facilities are created in the context of recreation, both active and passive, the subtle boundaries between them being natural both physically and psychologically.

In recognising nature's strengths, the creation of a process is proposed with nature, to heal, purify and reclaim the area into the surrounding built and unbuilt environment. It will aim to be attractive, informative, interesting and useful to the local and visiting community, and by its unique exhibition value, involving art, make its educational opportunities easier to access for all who use and visit it.

The concept is about creating confidence and pride in the future (our children) through the intelligent transformation and use of the site over time. The architectural proposition suggests and demands a reassessment of attitudes towards the future, but is firmly based on an awareness of the social and political context of Sodingen in which the project will be built. The concept of an Educational Woodland Park was approached by trying to understand and appreciate the site. There are three key components to this exercise: its physical characteristics and linkages, its surrounding social structure and its memories.

To summarise the site's physical characteristics it can be described as relatively flat, but higher than the surrounding ground to the west and north-west. The natural process of being covered principally by silver birch and appropriated in isolated pockets as allotments has begun. Its pollution has not yet been treated, either naturally or by man's intervention. The area is strategically adjacent to Sodingen town centre, to the south, and links to the landscape and recreational areas to the north-west. Geometrically, its structure precludes construction in certain areas of the site at this stage, and its water table, some few metres below the surface, receives pollution washed through by rainfall. Above the water table there is polluted mineral waste, from buildings and mining activities. Methane is being released from the ground, principally through controlled vents above the three vertical shafts.

From the above observations, four key factors can be appreciated. These are firstly that the silver birch will propagate and cover the site if left alone; secondly, there is a

'demand' for allotment space; thirdly methane release could be used more intelligently and finally, control of pollution into the water table needs to be introduced. In addition, the site offers the opportunity to study and research the ground pollution in a natural way, and maybe also experiment to explore new methods of ground purification.

The surrounding social structure The following presentation mainly results from an explorative survey of the population of Sodingen carried out by Ian Ritchie Architects. Similar to the whole of the Emscher region, Sodingen suffers from the consequences of deep structural change, especially in the form of high unemployment. A 'solution' to these problems can, so far, only be seen in early stages and different potential developments have to be anticipated as equally possible.

One result is a high percentage of older people. The high availability of universities (Bochum, Dortmund, Essen) has so far only helped to slow down the brain-drain. The integration of foreign citizens has not happened to a desirable extent; there are problem areas – perceived as such by the population – some of which adjoin the site directly such as Kantstrasse and Uhlandstrasse. Differing ideas exist within the population as to how these problems could be overcome and how the development of the old pit could affect these problems.

The town benefits from a well developed infrastructure; the possibilities that are offered by its situation within a polycentric agglomeration are appreciated and used by its population. It is well equipped with parks and leisure facilities (Gysenbergpark); this is perceived as the main 'trump' by the population. Nevertheless, there is a demand for additional easily accessible and useable parks and play areas. Especially women and the elderly sense increasing problems with the security of public spaces. The town is appreciated as home by a large part of the population. The advantages of a small town with village characteristics in combination with the proximity of urban facilities are well understood and used. The arrival of the Academy is generally welcomed; the level of information within the population nevertheless could be higher. There is undoubtedly an acceptance and an interest (possibly more passive) in an ecological improvement of the town and in the use of environmentally friendly construction methods.

Therefore the design of the site needs to take into account the interest in subjective and objective security through lighting, visibility, etc. All action should be accompanied by an open, intelligent and positive information policy. The site should be equally useable for all segments of the population to act as an integrative element. The population is interested in the Academy; uncomplicated interfaces should therefore be created between it and the public realm.

If the planning builds upon the existing potential of the town, while taking into account the above aims, the project offers a real chance to increase the attractiveness of the town.

There is no point in blindly burying the past history of the site. It is important to recognise it and appreciate any virtues and legacy it gives us. In the context of this site, there are

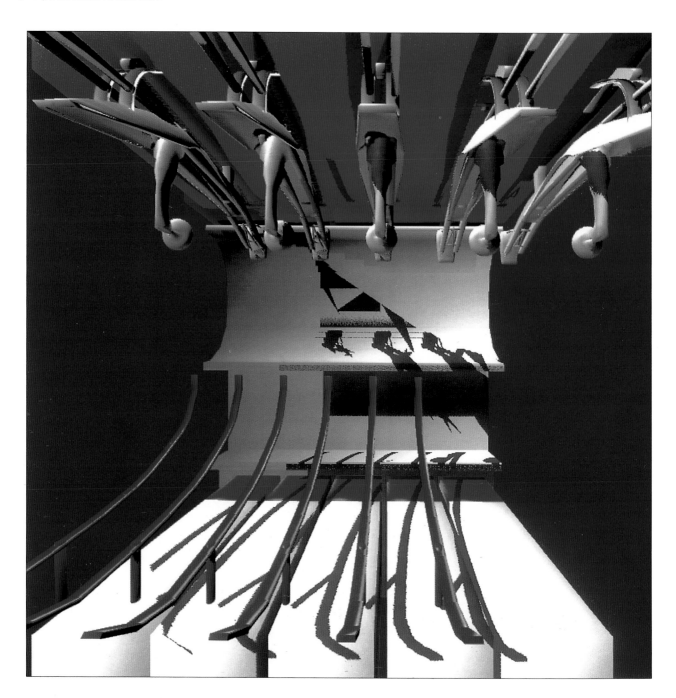

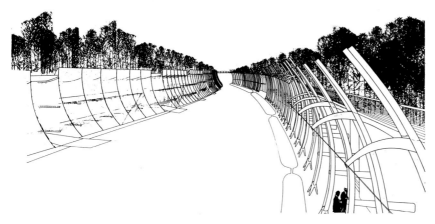

Opposite, from above: Abstract composition looking down on a section of the valley; Perspective showing the formation of valley by the glass cascade of the residential accommodation on the left and the Academy on the right; *From above*: View into a residential cell, from the service wall; Perspective of the valley; *Overleaf, clockwise from above left to centre*: William Paddock, 'How Green is the Green Revolution?', *Bioscience* Vol 20, No 16; Solar powered generator; Edges of the residential accommodation and the Academy; Built accommodation; Sunlight in the valley; Private domain; Public domain; Methane release pipe; Valley and the meandering river; Areas to be free of silver birches (showing Area 1 in white); Wind powered generator; *Page 89, above*: Installation by Andy Goldsworthy; Installation by Walter de Maria, *Centre*: Linear growth of the Academy in the valley; *Below*: Pedestrian and vehicular access; Landscape spaces

many people who have memories of the coal mining, and of course in time these people and their personal memories will disappear. Stories and myths will be passed on to future generations. The singular energy of methane and its potential use within the future Academy Park will serve as memory totems, thus giving visitors a physical reference to the site's past.

Interpretation – step by step

The wood The forestation of the site is predominantly allowed and encouraged to be silver birches. To do this the immediate control of pollutants filtering into the water table is necessary. However, this need not be across the whole site, particularly if other methods (natural and experimental) of dealing with this polluted ground are to be studied, and phased reclamation investment of the site is to be considered.

It is proposed to 'isolate' the north-east area of the site where silver birches have been developing over the last five to ten years. To do this, a 'bund wall' will be built. This consists of vertical clay 'walls' built into the ground, to surround the wooded area, which will isolate the ground from the water table. Scientific research will be able to take place within this wood.

The valley The valley is the 'first' clearing in the silver birch wood. This south-north curved valley begins at the edge of town, near the old colliery entrance and slopes down, widening out as it reaches the northern edge of the site. This topographical geometry begins the hierarchy language of density/intensity near the town, and openness towards the countryside, which will be reflected in the other elements of the architecture and landscape design. The valley will inform the design of the landscape to the east and west. It is the connection between the town and the public open space to the north and north-west of Sodingen, suggesting a nature route around Sodingen to the Volkspark in Herne. The valley, and route, is for pedestrians, cyclists and emergency vehicles.

This valley physically structures the Academy Park and will become a unique walk in the area. It will also become a special exit and entrance to the heart of Sodingen. Water will always be present in the valley. The design approach is that of land art, but respecting the economy of land movement and redistribution of the land within the site area.

The 'walls' To physically respond to the valley and spatially structure the Sodingen Academy Park 'radiating walls' have been proposed, one series emanating from the countryside, the other series from the heart of Sodingen. Sometimes they are single lines, and sometimes 'double' or twinned. The frequency of the walls decreases as they move away from the town. The walls are conceived as sculpture within the woodland, and could be interpreted by artists. For example, 'walls' towards the northern end to the site might be made by an artist such as Richard Long or Herbert Bayer; those more physical, but not yet suggesting boundaries by Walter de Maria, Andy Goldsworthy or David Nash; and those more physical, nearer the town, by Michael Heizer, Robert Heizer, Robert Irwin or

Richard Fleischner. These artists, among many others seek to represent a desire for a closer accord with the natural world.

The 'walls' are in reality a light framework which will provide support for many practical functions, eg retaining walls, storage, bridge walls, raised walkways, netting support for tennis courts, warm walls in allotments, windmills, etc, as well as spatially organising different activity areas with the park, such as play, allotments, car parking, etc. Pieces of 'wall' may appear as signs within the streetscape of Sodingen.

The clearings Apart from the central valley, other areas will be 'cleared' of silver birch to provide spaces for educational activities. These clearings will be discovered within the woodland, some large in area, others narrow and linear, possibly one horse-riding trail from the east through to the open country to the north. These clearings are to provide variety through the change in light within the wood. They are not all 'tamed' surfaces, only those specific to certain sports, for example, tennis. It is important that these areas, together with the more open area of the valley, should be very close to the unkempt wood, so that the tactile and visual qualities are immediate.

Built edges It is not envisaged that any built volumes will be physically apparent within the park, only surfaces and topology. The Academy can reinforce the feeling of 'density' in the valley towards the town end. The Academy accommodation has been placed 'within' and will create the 'built banks' (sides) to the valley.

The east side will be a 'glass cascade', the west side a covered walk. Together these two forms will reflect the natural shaping of the land by a meandering river. Landscape will be the first image with the Academy only discovered upon descending the valley. It will be denoted by the first 'bridge wall' crossing the valley, which acts as an open gateway.

The orientation of the Academy's teaching and recreational activities is predominantly north-east; and the residential rooms face south-west. This, and the placing of the buildings largely under the landscape is the primary decision towards low energy consumption for space heating and cooling.

Suppose that it were possible to invent an imaginary architecture. Suppose that we could think of architecture not as a thing, but as a process for perfecting the earth . . . if you think of most buildings as a process for perfecting the earth, most of them are simply unnecessary.
Arthur Drexter, Museum of Modern Art, New York

Spatial dimensions of the park The principal components of the architectural design: the wood, the valley, the walls, the clearings and the built edges create a three-dimensional woodland park, providing spatial diversity and richness. This design allows change to occur, both before construction and after construction, without affecting the basic architectural concept. In fact people's perception of the park will probably keep changing as natural growth and man's use of the park

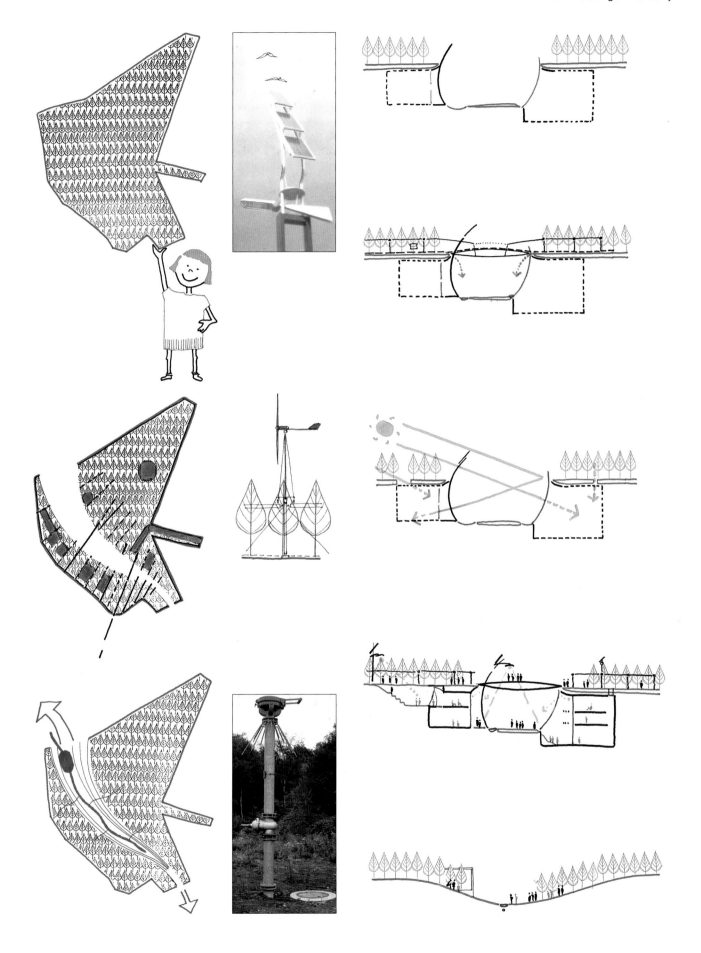

influence its spatial and physical characteristics. This is important to understand, and reflects a design which is not precious about itself, but in the larger sense is concerned about knowledge and the appreciation of change.

Public and private domains The park's spatial design suggests a natural hierarchy of public and private life. The public can walk anywhere over its surfaces. Where the general public cannot go is 'within' its surfaces.

The Academy is 'within' the park's surface, (as are the methane storage tanks). Sometimes, the public will be permitted to use some of the Academy's facilities; and this will change from time to time depending on the Academy's policy towards the public. These latter facilities are near the town end, and near the car park. Sometimes, parts of the surface will become special – eg ground investigation and monitoring – and inaccessible, but this too will change over time.

The simplicity of the designs means, in terms of accessibility, that without is the public domain, within is the private domain. The valley is the primary lit and safe route at night, with some of the 'twin walls', to the car park, and to the town, also lit. The lighting, the methane vent structures and the windmills become the first of a family of vertical sculptures all physically related to 'the walls'.

Growth The Woodland Park may well expand to the north-north-west, and it should certainly become more and more integrated with the landscape towards Herne. It will, fairly quickly, achieve an identifiable woodland volume. Sculptural lines are very much a framework to which and on which change can take place, both as screens and in defining change in the use of the land.

The Academy may become very successful and demands for expansion in the future have to be considered. The linearity of the 'valley' provides the opportunity to extend the residential and academic facilities to the north, and social functions to the south. Although less likely, it is possible that not as much space will be needed initially for the Academy. The architectural concept can also accept an initial phase of implementing the Academy. This would essentially follow the principles of residential to one side of the valley and the Academy to the other side.

Construction The first consideration is the land movement, followed by the protection layer of topsoil. The latter will need to be brought to the site. It is estimated that 90,600 cubic metres will be required (average cover 70cm) leaving aside the woodland area in the north-east part of the site. Recycling the existing mineral material overlaying the site, by using it as aggregate in the fabrication of concrete, has been considered. However, all this material will be used to help create the new land forms, prior to being 'sealed' by top soil. It is proposed that GGBS is used in the concrete mix, as it requires no further heat energy in its fabrication.

Energy The concept envisages energy production from the methane available, for both space heating requirements and electricity production. As and when newer, cheaper solar cells become available, and battery storage cells are more 'ecological', lighting and small power equipment will become used more. It is possible that experimental external lighting units could be installed initially, being expressed as vertical sculptural elements.

Higher levels of thermal insulation are envisaged to achieve better 'k' values than is currently the norm. The cost benefit to do this is viable. The concept proposes that all 'waste' material on the site is recycled on the site. This may not be completely feasible initially, but should be policy; for example, sewage waste can be treated on site. Any material not recycled during the early years would be compacted to minimise the frequency of collections. Wind, sun and biomass energy will be harnessed intelligently, and wherever valid will have an artistic function in the landscape.

Maintenance The concept design of the Academy buildings has an in-built low maintenance approach, and envisages, both by the choice of construction materials (for longevity and surface qualities) and the strategic routing and design of services (for easy pedestrian access – eg no use of motorised maintenance systems). The curved glass facade would be externally cleaned from the valley floor – cleaning is possible internally from the balconies.

The maintenance principles are based on creating a robust landscape and achieving self-regulating natural communities – with sensitive management rather than 'machine and chemicals' maintenance control.

The maintenance of man on earth is accomplished through the use of the energies incoming from the sun and from the stored energies of past evolutionary transformation of the planetary surface.

(*John McHale,* The Future of the Future, *1969*)

Access Pedestrian access from the site's perimeter is primarily from the existing main colliery entrance, and from new locations at the northern end of the valley and via bridge walls to the south-west. Vehicular access into the site from the east is limited to one area, incorporating the car parking requirements between 'the walls' and trees. This provides adequate access and proximity for deliveries and collections to the energy storage and plant, social areas and the Academy. Emergency vehicles (fire/ambulance) are able to drive down the valley, as the clearance height of the Academy entrance gate bridge is sufficient.

In order to create a better opportunity for the redevelopment of the area adjacent to the CO-OP, it has been suggested that this southern part of the Academy site is given back. This will also allow a better integration of this public area with the park by creating an identifiable link with a strategic 'strahlen'. Within the Academy buildings there are two lifts (social and teaching areas) for the use of the disabled and for heavier goods.

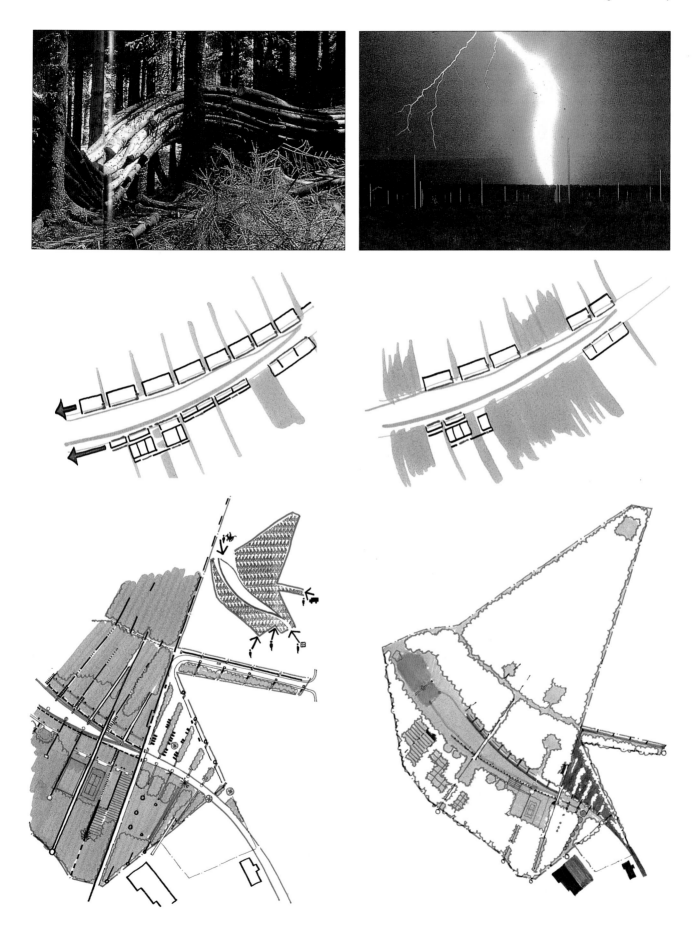

The architecture of the Academy Its appearance is discreet in the wider context of the park, yet it is powerful in creating the ambience of the southern part of the valley. The spatial ambience is initially created by the symbolic asymmetry of the valley. This symbolism refers to the dynamic dialogue between man's activities and nature, as well as the complex ecological process being one of turbulence, a fragile balance. The cascade of glass on one side of the valley gives it the impression of being 'sunny' and in turn reflects light to the 'shaded side'. The shaded side enjoys the early sun and though the day the rhythm of shadows changes, with the evening shadows being cast across the valley.

The external column supports of the Academy's learning and social accommodation create a covered arcade. The form of the columns responds to the load energy they are carrying and the transfer between them and the floors.

There are six key spatial experiences created by the simple concept of the linear architectural valley: the valley itself, with its asymmetry, running water and landscape; the covered external edge (arcade) to the Academy teaching and social areas; the enclosed relaxation and passive energy space in front of the residential units (this space is overlooked from the valley and internally from the residential balconies); the occasional bridge crossing and the long views up and down the valley; the 'vicolli' between residential groups connecting the wooded landscape with the valley; and finally, the valley edge walks along the top, providing splendid views of the valley and the opportunity to appreciate the change from an architectural valley to a natural one at the northern edge of the site.

Walking down through the valley (about a five-minute stroll), the visual and psychological perception of the valley's surfaces and edges will be slowly revealed. Through these surfaces, activities within will be seen – to the west, the social functions (ie restaurant/bar), the sports facilities (ie swimming pool) and the heart of the Academy's teaching areas. To the east, the residential units, lower recreational spaces (sometimes landscaped) and balconies can be seen. Residential privacy is provided by the largely translucent and insulated opening walls of the actual living spaces. The inner parts of the residential units are more private, such as sleeping areas and bathrooms.

The glimpses of the 'vicolli' are not only points of access in and out of the valley, but also visual reminders of the overall wooded landscape of the whole site. These 'vicolli' are defined by the sculpture lines and are of varying width, increasing as the valley becomes less built up. The spatial strength of the Academy's architecture comes from the three dimensions of space, and the desire that these spaces are diverse. The teaching and social accommodation have quite different spatial experiences from the residential accommodation. On the upper level, the communication route is constantly top lit. However, external gardens are created in the landscape, and here the route opens up, becoming a glazed conservatory and access to these gardens. This modulation of the route, both

spatially and in offering intermittent views out of the landscape, ensures an interesting environment for those attending lectures in different parts of the Academy.

The two main vertical circulation areas of the Academy are top lit, double height spaces and are reflected in the wider landscape by the prominence given to the two sculptural lines intersecting them.

The architecture of individual components The design approach can be summarised as: 'More From Less' and 'Form Follows Desire'. These two maxims are not contradictory. The former recognises that individual components should be made from the minimum amount of the chosen material, both physically and in the energy required to produce them, and also that this material performance should lead to each component performing more than one function (cf natural world). The latter recognises human need for delight in the shapes and composition of the built environment.

It is these two maxims which frame the creative process in the designs. For example, the Academy structure, the thin concrete panels in GGBS, will also integrate by their assembly, the air passages and thermal storage, and by understanding the fabrication opportunities and limitations, hand basins, shower floors and light fittings can be integrated. Another example is the columns, which support the Academy teaching and social buildings. These combine the structural column, lighting, handrail, support and bridge anchorage points and through their section and overall form, express a desire to be delightful and didactic.

Graphics The communicated image of the new Academy is an essential ingredient in the process of informing the wider public, and it is a function which is often underestimated. Graphics mediate between professional and public boundaries. The logo developed for the site and the Academy originates from the silver birch leaf, and achieves its final graphic form as representative of a young tree. It will, hopefully, communicate nature, learning and growth, pointing towards the future and creating a notion of confidence and friends.

During the preconstruction phase of the project, communication to the people of Sodingen, Emscher Park and beyond will be significant, and a logo is an important ingredient. It is obvious that further development is needed to identify the scope of the graphics materials which will be required. However, consistent with the maxim 'More From Less', the signage material within the park will be limited as much as possible, because profusion will become visual litter.

Landscape The objective of the landscape design is to allow natural communities of plant life back into the town. This can be realised by the re-establishment of woodland; the creation of water bodies and wetland areas by using collected rainfall; the development of meadowland communities; the natural establishment of varied wildlife. The objectives will be supported by low-key management. The ecological objectives can be integrated with human uses in order to provide: visual amenity (green infrastructure: woodland); screening (woodland and undergrowth) framed views; spatial variety (valley/clearings/routes) and movement.

Microclimatic benefits, such as shelter, shade, insulation, cooling and clean air, can also be gained by synthesising human and ecological goals. Educationally, scientific experimentation, exploratory play and plant nurseries are additional advantages. Furthermore, formal and informal sports activities, play, passive recreation and allotments will provide leisure benefits.

Areas The valley is to be carved into the site as the central spine of the development into which the buildings are to be set and over which the scheme's sculpture lines cross. The valley floor makes progression from hard urban form at the southern entrance to the site to open meadow with lake at the northern end. Running most of its length is a stream of water fed from small waterfalls at the valley entrance which lead first through hard edged urban water courses alongside building edges, collecting run-off and purified and waste water as they go, then through a transition zone between leisure and Academy buildings, to a rural area of meadow beyond. Here the stream falls to the soft edged lake at the open end of the valley. The water is then pumped up to the water bodies at the head of the valley to commence the journey down again. The valley forms the central throughway for the site with pedestrian and cycle routes leading the whole way alongside the stream.

It is proposed that the park be allowed to return naturally to woodland in which and through which a multitude of different activities can occur. Circulatory routes, open glades and variety in the nature of planting can allow for all the activities laid out in the design objectives.

The new woodland would be allowed to extend around all the boundaries, creating a minimum ten-metre-wide buffer zone. Vehicular access routes and parking would be screened by trees and the sculpture lines. The sculpture lines will also define the edges of different site uses, such as the nets around tennis courts. The landscape would extend over the roofs of all buildings, integrating (and insulating) the architecture. Sunken gardens will be formed as semi-private clearings in the woods, adjacent to seminar rooms, swimming pool and restaurant, encouraging a relaxed opening-out of the building accommodation into the park.

Animals are an essential part of the organic agricultural cycle, consuming scraps and providing re-usable waste of their own. The animal community would be allowed to establish itself within the wood and meadow areas of the park naturally.

A private walled garden (kitchen garden) is proposed, giving off from the kitchen accommodation, producing fruit and vegetables for use in the Academy and encouraging those who work in the Academy to feel an intrinsic part of the park's regeneration.

In order to preserve one of the site's best existing assets and to allow an extensive area for observation of natural

regeneration, it is proposed that the large area of existing birch woodland to the north-eastern side of the site be maintained. The area would have to be sealed by a vertical trench (to bedrock level) of impermeable material to its entire perimeter in order to prevent leaching of toxic material within the soil to surrounding areas which are to be improved or capped with loess (introduced vegetable soil). As an example of self-regenerating woodland on waste soil – as opposed to the newly created plantations on introduced loess – this area could fulfil numerous educational and research objectives. Additionally, it is proposed that this woodland provide a few circulatory paths for joggers and walkers.

The north-eastern corner is made up of existing agricultural land which could be utilised for the development of plant nursery and small maintenance base. This would support landscape maintenance of the Academy valley and roofs, and also provide an educational resource base monitoring natural and experimental pollution treatments of the soil.

The woodland will be planted and encouraged to propagate right up to the site's boundaries, but will be tempered in response to the variety of events along its borders. Allotments already surround the site perimeter to the west and such land use should be encouraged within the site as educational and leisure use of land for the local community. Annual vegetable crops, herbs, soft fruit and perennials can be grown with the assistance of site-produced compost and irrigation assisted by wind pumps.

Thick growths of trees are appropriate backdrops for the gardens of the adjacent proposed housing, and serve to protect the park from intrusion of future construction work. Moulding of the earthscape with banks to the south-west edge enhances this effect. The south-east corner of the site has been acknowledged as the meeting with Sodingen town centre, and it is proposed that this should be animated with more artificial interventions as a sculpture park.

Implementation and management The primary aim is to allow a self sustainable and self-regulating woodland. In the early stages, ecological landscapes can be labour-intensive to establish, therefore correct training and education of staff is very important with less reliance on machinery and chemicals and a more pragmatic approach required to the landscape's development than that adopted in a conventional park situation. However, with sensitive and minimum intervention management inherently productive and self-regulating communities can be achieved.

Areas left over from anthracite mining are generally high in sulphur, are acidic, are frequently unstable and compacted, suffer extremes of surface temperature and are low in nutrient and organic matter. Significant vegetation has established in the spoil – mainly *Betula* sp with occasional *Salix* sp and a herb layer of *Solidago* – but the lack of variety after a few years indicates the difficult conditions.

It has been recommended that loess should be used to cap the existing surface material, following earth moving operations which are necessary because of the toxicity and instability of the colliery spoil material (except north-east woodland area). As a first step, it will therefore be necessary to transplant all existing plant material of merit if it is to be preserved for re-use. It is proposed that a maintenance base complete with maintenance team, fenced holding area, planting beds, water and power supply be established on site prior to any earthworks and construction. An area has been identified for this at the north-east corner of the site, although additional holding areas for the transplanted material could occur more centrally to the site due to the temporary and phased nature of the works.

While earthworks, construction and vegetable introduction progress, the team can develop plant nurseries and seed beds 'growing on' native material for the planting phase. Efforts would also be concentrated on monitoring and enhancing the area of existing woodland which is to be retained and sealed. The programme of experimental and management work ultimately envisaged for this site must be instigated at this early stage if it is to be meaningful and as it would also lead to the ultimate design proposals for planting mixes. Following the completion of construction works, the formation of the finished water bodies and vegetable soil profile would be carried out in close liaison with the landscape management team in order to create the optimum environment offering individual planting areas. Compaction must not occur and good drainage is to be ensured. The incorporation of compost from the surrounding area during cultivation could aid establishment of a nutrient-rich soil and such recycling should be continued for all soil improvement.

Whilst lake edges, roof gardens and areas adjacent to the main access routes would require individually considered planting and greater maintenance, the bulk of the site would be covered by woodland planting. The main species is *Betula* sp. The early site experiments could suggest the final constituents of the planting, but an early indicative list might include: major woodland trees (for long-term climax community), nurse species (for fast growth but early thinning), minor woodland trees (for edging/flowering interest) and a shrub layer (for edging/banks/under-storey).

The opportunity to 'accelerate' the woodland park to create initially a more substantial woodland area is possible by grid planting in certain areas and hydraseeding in others. Equally, some woodland harvesting for on site use or the immediate neighbourhood is probable, in much the same way that other waste material is recycled on site. In addition, certain trees might be required to fulfil specialist functions in certain areas such as 'street trees' at the hard, urban end of site, while different species would be used at the water's edge and in reed bed habitats. Ground cover and climbing plants will be required in situations relating directly to buildings or banks. Grass and wildflower seed mixes could be hydraseeded over the areas of open meadowland to be created at the north end of the valley. Meadow hay would be cut twice a year and could be composted.

An educational natural environment would eventually become established, replacing the site's blighted industrial heritage. The approach should avoid the wasteful high energy input alternatives of flower garden and sterile mown grass, as prevalent in the traditional ornamental urban park.

Structural engineering Construction is restricted on the site for a number of reasons: methane sources (control vents) with exclusion zones; unstable sub-soil, otherwise requiring extensive treatment to permit building; substantial area of forestation; mud ponds and badly contaminated ground from mining operations. Following investigation and advice, Area 1 has been selected as the least problematic. Area 1 is a long narrow strip, which has helped to define the linearity of the proposal, (see p87, with Area 1 indicated).

The construction is proposed partially below existing ground level by excavating to naturally compacted ground. By partially burying the buildings, the physical impact of them is reduced. A large proportion of pre-cast elements would be used to minimise the environmental impact, by reducing the period of on-site construction. Furthermore by opting for pre-cast elements, capable of some flexibility in form and size, a series of components can be produced in reasonable quantities from the same mould, thereby reducing production and on site costs. This structural efficiency responds to the ecological philosophy of the park. The intention is to produce high-quality, self-finished, pre-cast components, both externally and internally producing in effect a high percentage of pre-finished surfaces.

Sculptural concept A single structural principle is applied to the construction of the three main building types, the residential units, teaching spaces and social facilities. The valley is to be formed by a process of excavation in area 1 where contamination is limited. Through a combination of 'cut and fill', with dynamic vibro compaction techniques to form a reasonable bearing stratum (layer) for the proposed buildings. The buildings will be constructed as a series of discreet blocks along the valley, separated by 'vicolli', allowing independent settlement of each block. By accepting this settlement, normal and necessarily costly (and time consuming) compacting of the ground is reduced.

Each group of units will be supported on an *in situ* reinforced concrete slab, with a stiffened retaining wall which will also creates the continuous service zone. The *in situ* slab and walls will create the 'structural skin' providing good overall stiffness to the section (schnitt) against localised settlement. Being *in situ*, the actual forms of the 'structural skin' can vary to allow the formation of varying size and length of buildings which will sit on them. The remainder of the structures is proposed in prefabricated elements, both in concrete and in steel.

The enclosures for the smaller units (residential, offices and seminar rooms) are to be constructed from GGBS concrete, reinforced with a combination of high yield steel and glass fibre; the steel providing the tension resistance, and the glass fibre providing excellent crack control (quality of surface finish) along with the possibility to form very thin and complex profiles (12mm). This will also allow the construction of sinks, shower elements, shelves, etc, elements within the non-loadbearing structural walls. Considering the units as stiff boxes it is possible to independently stabilise each unit and achieve thin walls and floors by efficiency in load distribution.

Furthermore, by separating each unit from the adjacent unit with the moment connections (necessary for tolerancing), voids will be formed which will provide all round acoustic separation, and a zone for the passage of air, allowing heat exchange through the floor slabs. The smaller units will be self-supporting, the lowest unit using 'tolerance feet' on to the *in situ* ground slab to provide separation and support. The other partitions (non-loadbearing) will be made of prefabricated concrete, steel and glass panels as necessary, additionally a series of other components can be developed to increase the variation in the final units. For the larger spans (social and some teaching accommodation) a more typically hierarchical structure is necessary, due to the desire to have both wall and column free space.

However, the same principle is applied with the wall used for the smaller units being replaced by a downstand beam. This downstand beam can be made to the necessary depth to suit the required span (from 12-20m). The section will be made more efficient by restraint to the compression flange by the slabs above. The beams carrying large point loads will then be supported by a pair of double columns (easing the structural connection) which bear directly onto the locally stiffened *in situ* ground slab. The roof and floor slabs are to be supported on simply supported beams acting compositely by continuous connections with the slab to form stiff 'T' beams. These will be supported on the *in situ* service fin wall and on the precast paired columns outside the building facade.

Stability to the floors is to be achieved by horizontal connections to the service wall and by the floors acting as full 'in plane' diaphragms. The partitions will be made in the same way as the accommodation units. The landscaped roofs, providing high thermal insulation, will produce higher loadings. In this situation, a second precast slab will be placed over the upper unit roof slab, capable of resisting the higher forces induced by this loading, and also creating a heat exchange void.

Energy The reduction of the energy demand is to be achieved through the positioning of the buildings and the form and construction of the buildings. The buildings will be positioned on both sides of the valley. The envisaged result is that the larger part of the external walls is protected from wind through soil and the solar energy can be collected and stored in glazed energy zones.

Therefore, in summary, the design of the buildings follows three aims: optimised thermal insulation, use of solar energy through storage and distribution, and energy-efficient fresh air supply through use of heat produced by the building.

The optimised thermal insulation is to be achieved by wrapping all the parts of the building which are in contact with the ground or external air with 200mm thick PU-slabs. The solar gain is to be achieved through south-facing glazed buffer zones. Buildings with an inner energy supply (heat generation through people, equipment, etc) for example the seminar rooms will have a north-facing external wall. Buildings with lower energy production and higher consumption, like the apartments, will open up to a south-facing glass hall.

Optimal thermal insulation is useless if it is not complemented with controlled fresh air supply. Special emphasis has therefore been put on the development of a ventilation and heating system which combines precise heat recuperation and flexible controls with minimal technological effort. This system will also be used to transport surplus heat to the coolers on the north side. The system will vary depending on the building type.

Type A (apartments) This type consists of the glass hall, the pre-fabricated living units and the lightwell in the back. Floors and ceilings of the units are to be separated by an air void (d = 100mm). This gap will be used as a combined surface-air heating system. On this basis, the building will work in different climatic conditions. In winter, from each bath/toilet area 40-60m^3 air will be extracted per hour (DIN 18017) directly to the outside through a system of ducts and a heat exchanger. This extracted air will be replaced by fresh air which is preheated by the heat exchanger.

This fresh air is then pumped through the lightwell into the voids in the floors of the living units. It flows through the floors to openings near the windows and then through the space itself before it is extracted through the bath/toilet area again. If required, this air can be heated through individual radiators in the void under the bath/toilet area. By placing them next to the bath, this area will be the best heated part of the apartment. By combining floor and air heating, a flexible temperature control can be achieved. Fast warming up periods, lower temperature requirements in the night and for unoccupied rooms, all help to save energy.

When the building is unoccupied the air can be circulated through the floors and spaces with the fan set on a lower speed. In transition periods, ie on a cold but sunny day, a lot of heat is stored in the glass hall. The external air fan can therefore be used to exchange air and heat. This fan is run, in these instances, with double air volume. This circulates through the ceiling void of the top apartment, a separate duct in the lightwell, and then upwards through the lightwell itself and finally through the floor/ceiling voids of the other apartments. The stored solar energy can thereby be used to heat the apartments. At this point the building does not need any external heat input.

In the summer, fresh air will be pumped through a separate duct in the ground. This air, cooled by the ground to temperatures below that of external air, will then be pumped through the floor/ceiling voids to cool the spaces. Air extracted from the bath/toilet areas will provide extra cooling via the heat exchange. At this point the fan will run at a higher speed. Air that is not passed through ventilation openings in the floor into the living spaces will flow into the glass hall, cool it down and rise through the open chimneys.

The hall will be cooled directly through a fresh air inlet at the bottom of the hall which ducts air through the stream. Therefore, two fans will be sufficient for the whole living area. The energy consumption of these fans is very low, since air is transported at low velocity (0.10-0.50 m/s) and natural buoyancy will be used where possible. In addition, there will be periods when the cooling of the building through natural buoyancy without the use of fans will be sufficient.

Type B (Academy) This type consists of the seminar rooms on the upper storey which will be closed off to the north with a thermally insulated external wall and to the south with a glazed buffer zone. Below the seminar rooms are to be the office spaces which will connect with a circulation zone in the north. Floors and ceilings are separated by air gaps as in Type A.

In winter, an air change rate of 30-50m³/h per person will have to be provided. This equals for the offices 0.5 and in the seminar areas 1.5 to 2.5 air changes per hour. For heating purposes these spaces will be run with 0.5 air changes. Unoccupied rooms will be switched off and held at a minimum temperature of 15°C by intermittent running of the system. The extracted air will be compensated for by the fresh air fan and the fresh air will be heated by a recuperating heat exchanger. The efficiency of the exchange lies at 85 per cent. The ducting of the air through the lightwell, the individual top-up heating and the air supply through the floor/ceiling voids will work analogically to Type A.

In transition periods, as for Type A, heat from the glass hall is to be used to heat the spaces through an increase of fan speed and opening of the circulation ducting. The extracted air from the seminar areas is to be separately ducted to the outside.

In summer the external air fan will suck cool air through a duct in the ground and pump it through the voids between floors and ceilings. The seminar rooms are to be supplied directly through the ducts in the circulation area. In extreme climatic conditions the cooling of the building will be feasible through the building's use of natural buoyancy without the help of any of the fans.

Energy supply As measurement over periods of approximately ten years has shown, there is considerable production of methane gas in disused coal pits. This gas, so far, has leaked uncontrolled into the atmosphere. Measurements for comparable pits have shown that one has to expect volumes of 10-20m³ per minute per shaft. The concentration of pure methane would be around 50 per cent if small quantities are gas are extracted or 20 per cent if large quantities are extracted. It is therefore proposed to collect the gas from the three disused shafts, to compress it and, if necessary, purify and store it. It could then be used (if necessary in combination with town gas) to supply the energy for the Academy. The most energy efficient form of heating plant is the combined heat and power plant which produces electrical energy and uses the surplus heat from exhaust fumes and cooling process to heat buildings. With an input of 100 per cent primary energy, an electrical output of 35 per cent and a heat output of 60 per cent can be achieved. Therefore a CHP plant has been proposed, using a combination of methane and town gas. Further studies concerning concentrations, quantities and general feasibility will be necessary before this strategy can be implemented. In the long term the diminishing reserves of methane should be compensated for by increased use of other forms of energy, preferably solar energy.

The CHP plant has to be sized to be able to produce for a basic demand, peaks will be catered for by an additional boiler (methane) and supply from the electricity grid. Generally one assumes a high period under full-load for the sizing of a CHP. This guarantees the highest cost efficiency in monetary terms. From the ecological aspect, a higher CHP load should be assumed. Part of the further planning, therefore, needs to be the establishment of these criteria.

As shown on the plant diagram, the hot water supply is also heated by CHP heat. The surplus heat from the CHP can be stored in hot water storage tanks and in the swimming pool. Only during periods of extremely low heat demand the surplus heat cannot be stored any more and will need to be given into the atmosphere through heat exchangers.

Water In this area three aims are to be followed: if possible all water collected on site should stay there; secondly, the demand for tap water could be dramatically reduced if rainwater from roofs and sealed areas, as well as treated water from showers, baths, basins and washing machines, is re-used; and thirdly, rainwater should generally not seep through polluted soil into the ground water.

To achieve these objectives, a combination of a collecting lake, a biological treatment plant and a system of Aquaplant reed beds is proposed. The grey water collected by this process is to be used for toilet flushing and the feeding of the stream. Toilet effluent can also be treated in this system. Sewage sludge produced could be integrated in the park.

The chance for such a system to be realised depends largely on negotiations with the relevant local authorities, but deserves to be discussed thoroughly.

Architects: I R Architects; Structural Engineers: Atelier 1; Service Engineers: Schmidt Reuter; Economists: Drees and Sommer

Opposite, above: Site energy sources and recycling – utilising the site methane, solar energy, wind and biomass, excess stored methane is to be transferred locally to provide energy to nearby buildings; Site water sources and recycling – utilising the new valley landscape to collect water from the site and buildings (wind driven water pumps, with power back-up, water storage, solar energy store and filtration beds); *Centre*: Type A (apartments) winter and summer; *Below*: Type B (Academy) winter and summer

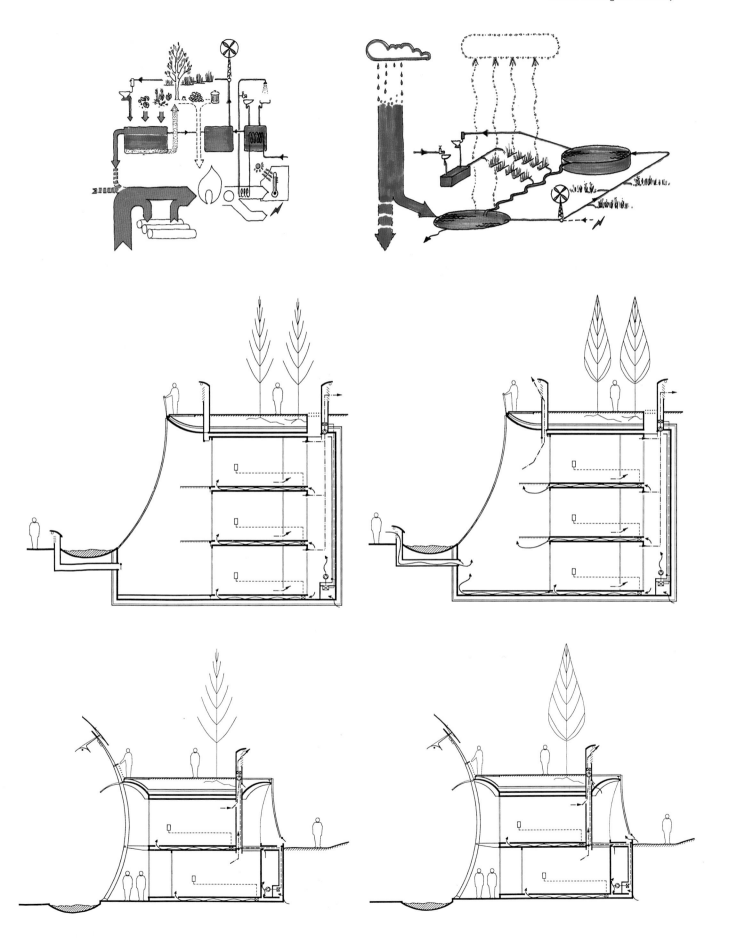

IAN RITCHIE

BIOGRAPHY

Dipl Arch (Dist) RIBA MCSD
Member of the Royal Institute of British Architects
Member of the Chartered Society of Designers
Registered French and German architect

Graduated from the Polytechnic of Central London (now University of Westminster)	1972
English Culture Teacher, Oita University, Japan	1970
Project Architect, Foster Associates	1972-76
Urban Design Lecturer, PCL (University of Westminster)	1973
Private Practice, France	1976-78
Tutor, Architectural Association	1978/81
Design Consultant:	
– Michael Hopkins Architects (SSSALU)	1979
– Ove Arup + Partners	1979-81
– Peter Rice (Shelterspan Fabric Structures)	1979-83
Chrysalis Architects, London (with Mike Davies and Alan Stanton)	1979-81
Principal, Ian Ritchie Architects, London	1981-
Director, Rice Francis Ritchie (RFR Design Engineering), Paris, with Peter Rice (Engineer) and Martin Francis (Naval Architect/Industrial Designer)	1981-
RIBA External Examiner, Humberside University	1985-89
Visiting Critic, Sheffield University	1986-88
Consultant Director, RFR	1987-
RIBA President's Medal Assessor	1987
RIBA External Examiner, British Steel Corp Teaching Project	1987-89
Chairman, RIBA Regional Awards	1988
Urban Design Review Board, LDDC, London	1990-93
RIBA External Examiner, University of Westminster	1990-93
Architectural Advisor, Natural History Museum	1991-
Workshop, Moscow Institute of Architecture	1991/92
RIBA External Examiner, University of East London	1991-94
Civic Trust Awards Assessor	1992
RIBA External Examiner, University College, London, Bartlett School	1993-
Ian Ritchie Architects, Germany	1993

AWARDS

UIA Student Award: Agora/Leisure	1972
International Aluminium Design Award, USA, SSSALU (prepared for Michael Hopkins & Partners)	1980
AD Architectural Design Award: Fluy House	1981
AD Architectural Design Silver Medal: Eagle Rock	1983
Plus Beaux Ouvrage Metallique, France (RFR)	1986
Laureat Concours Symbol France-Japan: Poiesis	1988
Iritecna Prize for Europe	1991
Financial Times Award Commendation: B8, Stockley Park	1991
Structural Steel Design Commendation: Reina Sofia Museum of Modern Art	1992
Eric Lyons Memorial Award, Europe: Roy Square	1992

EXHIBITIONS

UIA, Bulgarie (Agora/Leisure)	1972
Paris Biennale (Eagle Rock)	1982
Art of Architecture, ICA, London (Eagle Rock)	1983
Industrie et Architecture, Paris Beaubourg (La Villette)	1983
British Architects, Moscow (Eagle Rock)	1986
British Architects, Tokyo (Eagle Rock, Central House, Whitechapel, La Villette)	1987
British Week, Aarlborg, Denmark (Hermitage, Roy Square, Rainbow Quays)	1989
Salon International d'Architecture, Paris (Boves Pharmacy)	1989
L'Arsenal – Barcelona/London/Stockholm/Paris (National Maritime Museum of the Boat, Roy Square, Spitalfields)	1990
Light + Architecture, Ingolstadt and Frankfurt (Light Environmental Installation)	1992
Imagination, Moscow	1992
RIBA Art of the Process (Meridian Planetarium)	1993

RECENT AND CURRENT PROJECTS

Ian Ritchie Architects, London

Roy Square Housing, London	1987
New Meridian Planetarium, Greenwich	1988-
Pharmacy, Boves, France	1989
Glass Roofs, Louvre Museum, Paris (with OAP + IM Pei)	1989-93
Building B8, Stockley Park	1990
Ecology Gallery, Natural History Museum, London	1990
Reina Sofia Museum of Modern Art, Madrid (with Castro + Onzono)	1990
Business Research Building, Oxford Science Park	1990
Design Consultancy, Pilkington Architectural Glass	1990-
Cultural Centre, Albert, France	1990-
Bermondsey Station, Jubilee Line Extension, London	1991-
Limited Competitions, IBA Emscher Park	1991-
Academy Herne + Dortmund Housing, Germany	1991-
Experimental Greenhouse, Terrasson	1992
Leipzig Messe Glass Halls (with GMP)	1992
Ecole Maternelle, Daours	1992
Concours International d'Idées, Tremblay	1992
Invited Competition Carnuntum Museum, Austria	1993
International Rowing Club, London	1993
Geology Museum, London	1993
Mero Glass Canopy, Neanderthal Museum Competition	1993
Holy Island Competition, Scotland	1993

Rice Francis Ritchie (RFR), Paris

National Museum of Science, Technology + Industry, La Villette:	1981-85
Bioclimatic Facades, Entrance Roof, Rotating Domes, Robotics	1984-85
New Fabric Development with Brochier Aerospacial	1984-85
Lintas Suspended Glass Bridge, Paris	1985
Louvre Pyramid Structural Consultants	1985
Parc de La Villette Galleries	1985-87